A JOURNEY OF SELF DISCOVERY

JODI MARIE

"What I love about Loved, Healing, Whole is that Jodi Marie speaks in such a way that it puts courage in your heart and causes you to believe you can truly change as you put these tools into practice. Her conversational style draws the reader in and takes them on a journey of becoming. I highly recommend this book!"

—Teresa Carey
Wife and mother of three

"We all sometimes need a friend who's lived more life than we have to invite us for coffee and help us understand what the heck is going on—and more importantly, "How do I get through this?" Jodi Marie is that friend and Loved, Healing, Whole is her arm coming around you to say, "You're going to be okay and here's some truths that can help you." Instead of lofty goals to try to attain, Jodi weaves freedom-giving truth into real life in a way that makes it feels possible. Jodi hands us tangible, touchable tools that can help us make the journey from concepts to reality. Having worked for more than 30 years with women in prisons (the legal system ones and the religious ones) I can truly say that Loved, Healing, Whole holds authentic keys to freedom for every reader. Whether you're barely getting by or seemingly have it all together, enter her world for a bit and you'll be deeply changed."

—Allison Bown
Author of *The Image* and *Joyful Intentionality*
Founder of Grace Spaces Christian Coaching and Training
www.gracespaces.org

"This book is intensely personal, yet wholly relatable. It is a vivid story of trauma, recovery and healing. Jodi highlights the creative pathways God gave her to not only survive, but to thrive and become a stable person. These insights will be helpful to those working through traumatic wounding or for anyone trying to sort out the messiness of life."

—Rev. Ken Polsley
Former missionary, pastor, teacher, and speaker for Christian Healing Ministries

"Jodi Marie has not prepared a theoretical book of generic principles, but a potent toolkit that can be immediately applied to your life. Created and honed from lived experience and practice, each individual principle works in harmony with the next, equipping you to make real strides toward understanding what it is to live life as one "loved, healing, and whole." You hold in your hands an invitation to a life of ongoing transformation and freedom!"

—Anysia Derora
Author of *Exhilarating Journey* series

Loved, Healing, Whole: A journey of self-discovery
First Edition Copyright © 2023 by Jodi Marie

All rights reserved. No part of this publication may be reproduced, stored in a retrieval system or transmitted in any form by any means—electronic, mechanical, photocopy, recording or other-wise—without prior written permission of the copyright owner.

To contact the author: lovedhealingwhole.com

Red Balloon Press
A Division of Loved, Healing, Whole

All scripture quotations unless otherwise indicated, are taken from The Passion Translation , Copyright © 2018, BroadStreet Publishing Group, LLC
All rights reserved.

Edited by Meg Mittelstedt, Inkforge Book Coaching
Cover and interior design by NOTION Design Group
Typesetting by Kailey Kisabeth

ISBN:979-8-9888512-0-2

Printed in the United States of America

TABLE OF CONTENTS

Introduction	vii
Chapter 1—Loved Right Where I am 　　What is Love?	1
Chapter 2—Stay on the Side of Truth 　　What is True, Truth, and Divine Truth?	9
Chapter 3—Keep Your Side of the Street Clean 　　Pre-Company Clean-up	19
Chapter 4—Look Out the Windshield	29
Chapter 5—Wayfinding	35
Chapter 6—Oxygen Mask 　　Sub-tool: H.A.L.T.	43
Chapter 7—Pain Tolerance	53
Chapter 8—Redefine	65
Chapter 9—The Winning Hand	73
Chapter 10—Creating a Bubble	83
Chapter 11—Removing the Landing Pad	93
Chapter 12—Red Balloon	99
Chapter 13—Loved, Healing, Whole	107
Chapter 14—Welcome to Your Future	113
What's Next?	119
Influences and Resources	120

INTRODUCTION

I'm sitting here sick in bed as I write this—like *sick* sick. My throat hurts so bad that I feel like I am swallowing glass each time I try to take a sip of water. The pressure in my sinuses is so intense I feel like somebody punched me right in the nose. Worst of all, I can only sleep for 15 minutes out of every hour. I'm trying to take medicine every four to six hours, but honestly, I have no idea if I'm taking too much or too little. Time and days are running together like they do when the "sickies" hit.

I do *not* do well when I am sick—I know this, and everyone I know knows this. The pile of things I need to get done grows daily as I lay in bed, adding to what was an already overwhelming list. My kid is out roaming the house, fending for himself to stay alive, probably living off chocolate bars and chips. (Okay, I may be feeling *just* a little sorry for myself and exaggerating just a little bit. I know he'll be okay.) I also know homework needs to be done and dinner made, but yet I just *can't* be Superwoman today.

So, what better time to write the introduction to this book! I need *all* of these principles to get me through being sick.

I make a mental catalogue of the principles and how to apply them to this situation:

Oxygen mask: I can't help anyone else unless I can breathe—literally.

Stay on the side of truth: It is okay to let my kid be responsible for himself, and there isn't anything more important than me getting better right now. Realistically, if I don't rest and recover, I probably will get more sick prolonging the recovery process. Sometimes, truth is logic.

I am loved right where I am: My performance doesn't determine how much I am loved. I am loved on my "Superwoman" days just as much as I am on sick-in-bed days.

Look out the windshield: There is hope present, and I will get better. *Just give yourself a little grace,* I tell myself, and draw in the healing presence.

These principles—only four of the fourteen found in this book—have taken me two decades to actually get onto paper, but these fourteen are still the principles I rely on today. Part of the reason I am writing this book is to hopefully help others to live a life where they know they are "loved, healing, and whole." Another reason: I need these truths in my life daily to remain in the "loved, healing, and whole" mindset.

Remembering these principles seems to be the hardest part. So, now I have written a tangible reminder for myself—along with the grab-n-go cards to help keep them handy. I hope they help you, too.

I'd like you to consider this book a conversation between friends. Between me—sharing my insights and discoveries in the form of principles, resources, and stories—and you, the reader. Take them and find ways that work for you to apply them to your life.

To get to that conversational point, there are some things you should know about me, so that you'll understand where I'm coming from as I share throughout this book.

First, I believe in a higher power, and I choose to call that Higher Power God, Jesus, Holy Spirit, or sometimes Lord, Beloved, Savior or any of a myriad of other names that describe Him in the context of my relationship with Him. He is my Higher Power.

I understand this may not be your understanding or belief, and that is totally cool. I'm not here to convert you to my way of understanding or to argue theology with you. I've learned that keeping an open mind is important, as some of the most wonderful growth times can come out of conversations with people who have differing beliefs. These moments open a greater understanding of what is possible. I love to look at things from new perspectives. The saying is true: we don't know what we don't know!

Each day I strive to apply the principles that the Bible teaches and to be more like Jesus. He didn't judge people based on what they did; He is all heart. He loved, helped, healed, and befriended those whom society rejected, belittled, and even threw stones at. We don't always have to agree with someone's choices to love who they are as a person. I know what it feels like to be the outcast in need of love and compassion.

I say this, because my belief in God and desire to live according to His principles shows up in this book, in the stories I tell and in how I came to understand and use these principles. Also present in these pages you will hear the struggles I have faced to believe these things. If what I believe is going to be a stumbling block for you, then this may not be the right time for you to read this book.

Considering all this, let's talk finally about the basics of how I understand us as human beings. I believe humans are three-part beings comprised of body, soul, and spirit.

The soul is the "thinker" (mind), "chooser" (will), and "feeler" (emotions). The soul is deeply influenced by many things, including upbringing, beliefs, and experiences. It has an identity. It is influenced mostly by the world, the natural realm—what we take in through our senses.

Like the soul, the spirit also has influences. It is deeply influenced by Spirit, meaning a Higher Power. It also has an upbringing, beliefs, and experiences. It too has an identity. The spirit is influenced by heaven, the spirit realm.

Because the influences of the spirit and the soul are not always the same, they are not always in alignment. This is what it means to me to be "double-minded"—being out of alignment with, or feeling at war with, ourselves. It happens when these two influenced parts, the soul and spirit, contradict each other.

This is how I work it out:

I lived a lot of years only in my soul, connected to the world. It's where what I believed about myself was rooted. It was my story. Even though I'd read the Bible, knew scripture, and knew what I was taught, these two realities never seemed to line up. My story didn't have any evidence of what the Scriptures said or what I was taught they meant. It felt like a great divide. A separation of soul and spirit. I couldn't seem to reconcile my story on earth and the story in the Bible—my soul and my spirit.

I also had this life I lived in the spirit where I heard God, talked to Him, and walked with Him. I cried out to Him and prayed to Him. I fed my spirit by reading scripture, listening to Christian teachings, and journaling to Him—all starting at a very young age. I went to church and to a Christian school; my family prayed and read the Bible. I have been baptized with water and Spirit. I would "see in the spirit," meaning I had dreams and visions before I knew what they were called or what they were. I never really had what some consider a "conversion" moment; I have just always believed. I can't remember a time in my life when God wasn't a part of it. So, this was my other story—my spirit story.

In my earthly life in the world, I was hurt and betrayed by those I loved and who I thought loved me. I experienced violence and being violated. I became a drug addict and lived on the streets. I was abused in more ways than I care to ever look at all at once, because I couldn't handle it. I practiced witchcraft and played with spells. I stole, lied, and broke the law several times. I have even done jail time. You name it, and I probably did it.

All of this I did while also crying out to God, hearing Him, and believing He existed—even if what I experienced didn't look and sound like what I knew about the Bible. (I am not slamming the Bible, scripture, church or teachings. I am just explaining a little about where I came from.)

Two stories, one person.

I was living in my soul, with a spirit, all in one body. Three parts, one person. I grew up very confused at all the hurt, yet I also experienced these reprieves of peace that surpassed understanding. These occurred in glimpses of moments that I didn't really understand.

"Where's the story beyond the Cross?" I wondered. "Where is the evidence of the resurrected life that the Bible talks about?"

Eventually, I got sober, got off the streets, went through a ton of healing and even began to help others. Yet there was still this gap, this chasm, between my story on earth in the natural and my story in heaven in the spirit.

That's when I began to learn about living in my true identity. It was also when another layer of the battle between my natural story and spirit story began.

As I began to learn how I was known in heaven (which is my spiritual story and my spirit identity), I began to explore who God created me to be. This was very different from the person the world had led me to believe that I was.

This revealed gaps between how I was known in one story in the natural, versus the story in the spirit that I was learning. Yet for every gap, there would be a new experience of who I really was and who Jesus really was.

This book is about the principles I have learned that have helped me fill in those gaps along the way. I am not a scholar, a pastor, nor a theologian. I am a lay person who has walked this earth in relationship with a big God. I haven't arrived; I don't have the answers. I just "get" love, healing, and wholeness a little more now than when I first started my journey. Now I'm sharing some of the tools that have helped along the way.

It has taken me decades of healing in layers and a heart to see others be free in order to come up with the chapters in this book.

When you are first introduced to this book, I suggest reading through it once. Then pick your favorite principle—the one that hit your heart the most—and just camp there.

Don't think you are going to get it in one pass-through.

This isn't that kind of book.

Remember, it has taken me more than 20 years to come to some kind of understanding of how to use these principles and then write them. I am still unpacking, still learning, still applying and yes, even still forgetting to use them.

So, take these principles and make them your own. Don't look at them as a quick-fix formula or instructions for life. Instead, see them for what they are—the skills I've learned along the way that have helped me learn who I am. They're shared from my heart to yours with the hope that they will help you as you discover who you are on your own journey.

CHAPTER 1

RIGHT WHERE I AM

The sound of the waves crashing on the shore. The smell of the salt in the air. The clear starry night above and the sand beneath my toes. This is home—not this house I now sit in front of, so full of rejection and fear. No. The beach is my home now. The streets.

But where else can I go? I can barely walk. Pain grips my stomach every time I move. Standing up straight makes me vomit. Even the drugs and alcohol aren't bringing relief, and at only 16, I have no money and no transportation. It's also the middle of the night.

I need help and quick, I tell myself.

I know I need to go knock on the door of this house where I used to live—this house that has held so much pain for me. I know I need to ask for help. But my last memories of being here fill my mind. Yelling, slamming doors, packing my things and leaving. It feels like a lifetime ago, but still so vivid.

My mind is screaming at a God I barely believe in: "Tell me I will be okay!" Tears stream down my face as I sit here all alone, waves crashing on the shore like thunder. "Where are You when I need you? Help me! Are You even listening?"

I can't handle another rejection, not now. I'm too weak. I would rather die than face another rejection. I got myself into this mess; I have to get myself out.

God probably isn't even listening. Why would He now, when He hasn't so many times before? I mean, why *would* He? I haven't exactly been speaking kindly to Him. I haven't been honoring; I'm not pure or innocent. I just have no one else to turn to, and He is my last hope.

Suddenly, out of nowhere, I see the brightest, most brilliant, longest-lasting shooting star streak from one end of the sky to the other.

In shock, I wait, telling myself it must just be a night where there are a lot of them. Yet I see nothing else. And strangely, I *know*. I just *know* in that moment that all will be okay. No matter what happens, I will be okay.

Heart racing, I stand and walk slowly to the door. I stare at it for a second, feeling small.

Knock, knock.

Maybe no one will answer.

I ring the doorbell and the door opens.

"Mom, I'm sick. There's something wrong."

She looks at me, and I think I see compassion in her eyes.

"Go up to bed—we can talk about it in the morning," she replies.

For decades, I have replayed that moment—the moment God moved heaven and earth to speak to me in a way I could hear. I know beyond a shadow of a doubt that God visited me that night via a shooting star.

So, did my world turn right-side up that night?

Nope.

Did I get off the streets? Get a job? Get sober?

Nope, nope and nope.

But God knew that, and He still sent a star shooting across the sky. He still loved me right where I was.

And did you hear some of the things I was thinking at that moment? *Why would He help me? Me, a lowly teen, a street kid.* I was far from "holy" and couldn't even spell righteousness. I didn't know what honor was, or faith. I didn't know what I believed in. Yet there it was, that shooting star, and there He was. And I knew it was Him.

I have asked for that same scenario from Him a thousand times and it has never happened again. Yet the memory of that moment has stayed with me, carrying me through all the times I have jammed myself up since then.

***

Why do we judge so harshly? Why do we criticize, blame or shame? He always has and always will love us right where we are. And He also loves us so much that He doesn't leave us there.

I can't even begin to tell you how much I have learned since then about God and His love for me. But God *knew*. I didn't, but He did. He knew who I was, what I was capable of and who I would become. He knew the pain and the heartbreak I carried with me onto the streets—the pain that no one else knew or saw.

I could see only the fear I was running from and the fear I was running towards. When others saw only a rebellious street kid, God saw my perseverance, my grit, and my tenderness.

I am not in any way saying I was right in how I ended up there that night, or that what I was doing out there was justified. Or even that anyone else was wrong. What I am saying is, *He was there*. Right in the middle of my mess, showing up and loving me right where I was. He is also still loving me right where I am, every single day.

What is Love?

I feel like now is probably a good time to give my understanding of what love is, in order to bring clarity as you read. I will also say that, at the time the above story happened, I didn't have as much experience of this definition of love as I do now.

As I have more experience of love (as I understand it now) the above story also becomes more meaningful. That's what real love does. It heals the past along with the present and future.

I derive this definition of love from what is called the "Love Chapter" in the Bible: 1 Corinthians 13, verses 4-8.

To me, this explanation is like the baseline of an EGG. It helps me to clarify what love is and what it isn't. If I'm too high off the baseline of what love is, or too low, my relationships with others tend to suffer. How I feel about myself can also suffer, creating tension. It's not a perfect analogy, but it helps me, so maybe it'll help you.

I will also add the disclaimer that this isn't to be used to judge others on their definition of love, or to judge their heart. This is to explore *our own* definition, experience and heart—and possibly, to even redefine what love is.

Love is patient; love is kind; love is humble. It rejoices in the truth. It always protects, always trusts, always hopes, always perseveres. Love never fails. Love is a safe place of shelter, for it never stops believing in the best for others.

Love does not boast; it does not envy; it is not proud or self-seeking. It does not dishonor others. Love is not easily angered; it keeps no record of wrong. Love does not delight in evil. Love doesn't traffic in shame and disrespect. It is not easily irritated or quick to take offense. Love never takes failure as defeat, for it never gives up.

(I want to note here that I have pulled this together from different versions of the Bible and tweaked it some. It may seem repetitive; however, I quite enjoy a good list of superlatives to expand the understanding.)

When I talk about love, this is the baseline of what it is. A good baseline helps us to quickly recognize the ups and downs of what love is and what it isn't.

Now, I am nowhere near perfect at loving like this but, like I said, this is a good gauge for where my heart is and how I am loving. It also lets me know *how* I am loved right where I am. This is the kind of love that is right here with me, right where I am.

You are Loved Right Where You Are

For your two stories (soul and spirit) to come into alignment, and for those gaps in identity (between who others have told you that you are and who God says you are) to align, it's important to understand that you are loved. Right where you are. Just as you are.

No matter what your situation and circumstances look like, you are seen and known and loved. Not just "loved" the way we talk about it in society today, but loved in that 1 Corinthians 13 sort of way.

Loved in a God-way that is not proud or selfish or envious. Not a love that compares you with others to see if you are worthy. Not easily angered and not like a record-keeper of your wrongdoing, hoping that you'll do enough good to wipe out the bad. The kind of love that doesn't delight in the evil in your life. Love that doesn't manipulate you with shame and disrespect. Love that is not irritated with you nor offended by you. He loves you with a love that is perfect and complete, a love that never fails and never gives up.

Whether you believe in Him or not, or accept His love or not, this love is there, nonetheless. He doesn't need you to believe in Him for Him to believe in you. He also doesn't need you to be ready and waiting in order for Him to move heaven and earth on your behalf, so that you can say with confidence, "I am loved, right here, right where I am."

Stop for a second. Breathe. Let this sink in.

RIGHT WHERE I AM

Remember This Principle When….

- You are feeling unloved or unlovable.

- You are feeling worthless.

- You feel no one can love you because of your mistakes.

- You may think, "No one would love me if they really knew me."

CHAPTER 2

STAY ON THE *side of truth*

I'm frozen in place as I hear a voice calling out to me. Chills run down my spine. "Hide in the closet, quick!" I tell myself. Footsteps come down the hall towards my room. Closer, louder. I close the doors of the closet behind me quietly. I will myself not to make a sound. Heart racing. Shallow breathing. Body tense.

"Wake up, you're okay. I'm right here." A gentle hand touches my shoulder.

Fight or flight kicks in. *Where am I?* I wonder.

I am 30 years old.
My mom lives on Anna Maria. I have three brothers. I have nieces and nephews.
I work at a sign company.
I no longer live in that house.
I am in my bed, not hiding in a closet.
I have been sober for five years.

I can sometimes get lost on a dark path, one where a thought, situation or memory can lead me to a place I don't want to go, and keep me there longer than I want. I have felt so lost at times like these or when nightmares come, and this recitation was the only thing I knew to do to find my way back to where I really was. It was kind of like walking myself out of the past and back to the present-day.

I call this tool, "Stay on the Side of Truth." I don't always remember to use it initially; however, I'll remember to use it eventually. I'm getting quicker, but it's not instantaneous yet. I think that's pretty normal though. Sometimes it takes friends to remind me. We all need other people.

As I began to heal, this tool grew with me. As I began to learn my identity, the truths I would recite became more internal and less external.

I remember when I was going through an unexpected, uprooting life experience, some of the PTSD symptoms started to resurface. I was on the phone venting to a friend about all the things I feared, and all of the things I didn't think I could do on my own. I feared I would end up on the streets again, that I would lose my son, that I couldn't live alone, that I couldn't protect myself—I mean, for like an hour, I just let all the things in my head spill out in one long, rambling sentence. I was grateful that my friend just let me purge it all and listened (which isn't always easy to do).

When I was done, spent, and crying, she said, "Stay on the side of truth."

I yelled back, "I don't even know what that means!"

So, she went down the list of all the things I feared, but that weren't true about me or my situation anymore. It wasn't anything I didn't know already—it had just been momentarily lost above my cloudy sky. It was up there where the sun was, but where I wasn't.

Her reminders created a break in the clouds just long enough for me to see the light.

I'm not saying it caused some miraculous glory falling from heaven to turn everything around and then I was all good. But it was enough of a crack that it sealed up a resolve in me to change course, to remind myself that I was stronger than I thought. That truth was what was real—not my fears, not the PTSD returning in full force, and not my survival mode. My past failures *weren't* set in motion to repeat themselves.

I remembered that I had friends, people who loved me and who had my back. I had a relationship with an amazing God who had carried me through so much, and He was still right there. He had loved me right where I was before and didn't leave me then, and so He wouldn't leave me now, either. I had my son and no one was going to take him from me.

Do you hear all of the truth that I had to remind myself of?

It was true that I had been an addict, but the truth was, I was 18 years sober at that time. It was true that I was deeply hurt, but the truth was that I was also deeply comforted. I was grieving, but joy would come again. I wasn't on the streets. Instead, I had a place to live, food to eat, and love enough to help my son.

It was okay not to be okay, because it was true that I wasn't okay. I was hurt and to deny that would mean denying my soul the healing it needed. But the truth was that my spirit hadn't changed and my identity in Christ hadn't changed. I could hang onto that truth, even if I didn't feel it.

The truth was, "This too shall pass," as so many other difficult circumstances had passed.

Was I heartbroken, sad, grieving? Absolutely. What I *wasn't* was lost and alone, with no one there to help me. I didn't have to do this on my own, because I wasn't on my own.

Now, there was a choice involved: I had to choose to accept the help. Never forget that you have the power of choice.

"Staying on the Side of Truth" sometimes means knowing what the truth is, even when it isn't felt. It also means that eventually, after I stay on the side of truth long enough, the truth becomes my reality.

True, Truth, and Divine Truth

There are three definitions I want to add here to clear up any confusion with what I am talking about.

There is what is "true."
There is what is "truth."
And then there's "divine truth."
Let me break it down for you how I break it down for myself.

What is "True"?

I am sure everyone has experienced a conversation where you, and someone who experienced the very same moment, remember the things that occurred in two very different ways.

This would be what is ***true*** for each person. It doesn't mean either person is right or wrong. It's what is true for them from that moment that they remember.

What is true can be subjective. It's rarely objective. It has gone through filters and may not come out the same as it went in.

For instance, two people can witness a car accident and recount it differently. Two people could see the same vehicle as two differently-colored cars, depending on the light, the angle, distance, or even due to color blindness. But what they see, to them, is true.

What is "Truth"?

The *truth* may be that they are *both* wrong. It may be that they are both right as well, and perhaps the car was multi-colored or has a coating on it that makes it look different from different angles. The truth is, they don't know and they may never know. Now at this point, they can choose to argue that they each know the truth, but in fact, they don't.

This is how someone can get stuck in "what is true" versus "what is the truth." It's perhaps true that one person saw a red car and the other one saw an orange car, but that doesn't make either perspective *the* truth. The truth could be it was a brick-red color with a pearl coating that the sun was shining on, which made it look different to each observer.

What is "Divine Truth"?

God. Simple answer.

God's perspective is Divine Truth and there is nothing true or any truth that precedes it or that can change it. What God says is the trump card,
every
single
time.

Divine Truth is the truth that I'm striving to stay on the side of.

Sometimes it takes me a while to get there though, and that's okay. I may start with **what is true**:

I have too much debt and not enough money.

Then I go to **what is truth**:

I am okay though, because I have a roof over my head, I can feed myself and my son every day. It may be ramen, but it's food. I can also cut back some places to make money stretch.

Then I look for the **Divine Truth**:

My God will supply all my needs. The amount of money I have doesn't make me a lesser person. My Father in heaven gives good gifts and takes care of me. I am rich in love, joy, peace, and kindness—a currency that never ends. I have come from worse and have had less and the Way-maker made a way. I am strong and courageous. Patience will help me find a way.

My "what is true" and my "truth" are changed by Divine Truth.

What may be true isn't always the truth, and it may also be that it hasn't yet been subjected to Divine Truth, which has the power to change, uplift and renew what may have been true. In the same way, just because something may have been "true" about you in the past doesn't make it "the truth" about who you are.

I no longer have the nightmares like I did or wake up forgetting where I am, and I no longer have to remind myself of where I live, where my family is, or how old I am. Yet I do still wake up and remind myself that it's a new day. A new dawn. A new second. I do wake up and remind myself that I am loved right where I am, no matter what the day may bring. Sometimes I even run down the list of those who love me and whom I love.

That's what truth does. The bonds of the lies begin to break, like the clouds break after the storm to allow the sun to begin to shine again. In the middle of the storm, the sun doesn't cease to exist, just like in the storms of life the truth doesn't cease to exist. I just have to choose to remember that the sun is there, and eventually I will see it and I will feel its warmth.

STAY ON THE *side of truth*

Remember This Principle When….

- You are feeling under a cloud and can't see the sun.

- You are believing a lie about yourself.

- Your circumstances are dictating how you feel about yourself.

- You need to make an important decision.

CHAPTER 3

keep your side OF THE STREET *clean*

O sweet Starbucks, thank you for always being nearby. How I love to sit at your table, all jacked up on your caffeine, while I watch the circus of my life play out. You help me get all riled up, and pretty soon I find myself hollering on the phone at a friend.

Why am I even doing this? Getting all shaky and jittery because I feel like no one ever listens to me. Ugh.

You see, as I'm writing this, I currently have a situation where someone keeps bumping up against my boundaries and getting butthurt. Then I get butthurt because I am bumping against their responses, and because I'm having to enforce my boundaries so firmly.

Playing bumper cars with people like this is never super fun to navigate. I think the world is trying to show me something! (Insert eye roll emoji here.)

So here I am, looking at my side of the street thinking, *It needs a clean-up*—and probably also thinking some other not-so-nice things that I will not put in print because they would make my mother blush.

So, how do I remedy this?

Quite honestly, the first thing I did was I call my friend to vent, which is my go-to when I am butthurt and I want someone to agree with me. I said, "I knew I should have written about 'keeping my side of the street clean' before now!" Well, here I am, backed into a corner where I have to apply this tool, so I may as well write about it.

Here's what I'm pondering. For starters, healthy boundaries are good, but being hypocritical about them isn't. This needs to get cleared up first, no matter how hard it is to look at it. So, I have to apply the same standard to myself as I hope for from others. That's what this tool is all about: keeping it clean.

Just because it's hard to do this, doesn't mean that I should change my boundaries or that I should ask anyone else to change theirs. Their boundaries are their "side of the street." This tool is all about keeping your *own* side of the street clean, and not worrying about what is on the other person's side of the street. That's for them to deal with.

"Keeping your side of the street clean" is a principal I have been using since I was in the early stages of recovery. At that time, it didn't have a name—not until Holy Spirit tapped me on the shoulder one day.

I was being coached by a wonderful couple during a time when I was in a rough relationship and needed help. They had me look at "the love chapter" in the Bible, 1 Corinthians 13, that I referenced back in Chapter One. They asked me to look at this list of what love is and tell them which attributes of love I did well and which ones I struggled with.

As I thought about this, I realized I had been making a list of all the things the other person had done wrong, and I was using that as reasons to justify why I wasn't always "loving."

That's when the Holy Spirit "tap" came. "This is about cleaning up *your* side of the street. Love keeps no record of wrongs." At that moment, I had my answer for the coaches about what I needed to work on—along with a long list of expletives I let out at this realization! The record of wrongs I was keeping was both preventing me from loving others *and* from receiving love.

I can't clean up someone else's side of the street. What I *can* do is communicate my boundaries and then let people do whatever they are going to do in response. I can also forgive, which is a big part of keeping my side clean. I should use compassion, honor and respect while doing this, of course.

If I am getting mixed signals from someone, then it's on me to decide what I need to do for myself to keep my side of the street clean. I can't wait for someone else to clean up my street, or to clean up their side *before* I clean up mine—that's just adding pettiness to my side of the street, and I'll only have to clean that up later as well!

For instance, I quit drinking a long time ago, so I have some pretty strict boundaries about that—like no alcohol in my house when I am the only one there. My friends can come over, they can have drinks, but they have to take whatever is left back home with them, or pour it out and put the bottles into the recycling bin.

I don't hide from anyone that I am in recovery, so everyone around me is always aware. I don't even take cold medicine or mouthwash with alcohol in it. I am even cautious about the flavor of alcohol in food, even when it has been cooked out. I have a whole list of things that I do and don't do to keep me on the wagon and moving forward.

Still, some people are like, "It's been 21 years—why are you so strict with yourself?"

My answer? "Because it has worked for 21 years!"

This is an example of boundaries, rules—or call it wisdom—that I use to keep my side of the street clean and take care of myself.

Some people get butthurt that I keep such strong boundaries around drugs and alcohol. It's okay that they get butthurt; that's their side of the street. But I don't compromise my sobriety; that's my side.

When I am having a weak moment, my friends remind me of my boundaries, why I have them, and how they have worked for me for so long. They remind me that now wouldn't be the time to test them and see if I can "loosen up."

I do sometimes get hurt when someone doesn't want to do something with me or get to know me because I don't drink or don't go to certain places. But that is my side of the street; that's what's under my control. That's where I have to let others make their choices and let them be who they are, rather than to try to change their mind about me. Usually, neither person is right or wrong, just different. We all have the freedom of choice.

Sometimes, while I'm looking at what may not be clean on my side of the street, I also need to stay on the side of truth. When my side of the street gets dirty because of something I've done, I have the tendency to beat myself up. The self-talk can go something like this: *If someone else is hurt because of something I did, it must be my fault, right? And if I am hurt because of something someone else did, maybe my hurt isn't valid, because I must not have communicated well or I must have given the wrong impression.*

This is where my side of the street can get really dirty. I allow shame and condemnation to enter in—and then the next thing you know, I have a Starbucks in my hand and I'm sitting on my side of the street, over-caffeinated and not thinking straight. And then the monkeys show up, and the next thing I know, it's a three-ring circus of self-condemnation and not staying on the side of truth.

So, take my word for it—it's okay to correct things, to adjust or to go back to talk to the person if you need to. But hear this: there is no need to reject yourself or someone else when all that's needed is a slight correction.

Correction is NOT rejection. We can correct and clean up our side of the street while at the same time neither rejecting ourselves, nor our boundaries, nor someone else.

If someone feels rejected by this, that's their side of the street, and it's up to them to keep it clean.

Remember, we do this with honor, love, and respect. Not when we are mad, angry or trying to justify.

Sometimes people are just going to get hurt when they run up against our boundaries. We all have the freedom of choice. We can talk about it or let it fester—it's a choice. They have the choice to clean their side of the street—to talk it out and not let stuff fester.

I love the saying, "You do you and I'll do me." We are all different and unique. There is freedom in being ourselves and letting others be themselves and being able to celebrate each other as individuals.

This isn't a license to throw shade on another's side of the street. Cleaning up our side doesn't mean we put the blame on the other side or tear someone else down because we think this will make our side of the street look clean. That's just playing dirty.

Keeping our side of the street clean is about taking responsibility for ourselves. When we start to take more responsibility for others than we do for ourselves, we dirty both sides of the street. We can care about and love others. We can have compassion, be there for them, and be willing to help them. But we can't take responsibility for them or their choices.

If something is wisdom for you, that doesn't necessarily mean it will be wisdom for others at this point in their lives. We aren't all wired the same, nor were we meant to be. That's why we each have our own side of the street. Like me with alcohol, it isn't wisdom for me to drink, but I don't assume that means it isn't wisdom for everyone.

Pre-Company Clean-Up

How many times have you not had people over to your house because it was a mess and you felt self-conscious? Or, perhaps you've gone to someone else's house and judged how clean or dirty it was?

Now apply this tool to those scenarios.

Go dust off the cobwebs in your own house and don't worry about someone else's. They are capable of choosing to clean their own house. If you can't be in relationship because of a messy house, then don't.

The place to begin is by asking yourself, "Why is a messy house stopping me?" Is it shame, fear, pride or just a healthy boundary?

That's really about your side of the street, not theirs.

Also, when you're cleaning up—whether it's your house or your "side of the street"—take it step-by-step. One area, one room, one closet at a time. Don't overwhelm yourself.

Just remember, don't reject yourself in the process of cleaning up your side of the street. Don't get mad or, for example, feel like a failure, because you are, say, writing a book about "keeping your side of the street clean," while simultaneously realizing that your side of the street is a mess. (Just hypothetically, of course!)

Just humble yourself, clean up your side of the street and be grateful you have a wonderful tool to help you do it. Instead of—again, completely hypothetically—acting like a hoarder of negative emotions while sitting butthurt at Starbucks, internally wailing, "Send in the clowns, 'cause this is ridiculous!"

keep your side
OF THE STREET
clean

Remember This Principle When….

- You feel ashamed of something you've done.

- You feel slimed by a boundary violation.

- You are learning to apply boundaries.

- You are tempted to justify yourself or blame someone else.

CHAPTER 4

LOOK OUT THE *windshield*

Ears on alert, listening for dangers that may be lurking. Eyes wide. Sweat-drenched sheets tangle around me. *Why can't I sleep?* reverberates through my thoughts. My roommate snores, sound asleep in the next room.

Glass shattering, a broken picture frame lies on the floor. Blood tickles as it drips down my leg. I'm fighting to get free. I reach down and grab my leg, but feel only a scar. I am safe now. *No, I'm not!* The battle in my mind is on an endless loop. *Run!* I have to get out of here.

Memories, like shadows of trees, dance on the wall. *I can't take it! It's too much!* I grab my keys from my dresser. Humid air and the smell of farm animals hit me as I sprint to my car.

Turning the key, it's as if I am unlocking the door I'm trapped behind. The engine comes to life—the sound of escape.

On the back-country road, dust in my wake. Music blaring, me screaming. Cursing at the monster who is only in my mind. "You stole my freedom! You filled me with fear! You were supposed to help me, but you scarred me for life!" The wound that never really heals. The mark of evil. "Why do you get to go on with life while I suffer this tragedy over and over!" I'm trapped behind a wall of fear that follows me.

I keep my eyes on the rearview mirror. *Am I being chased?* I keep checking if the darkness from my mind is following me.

Holy Spirit asks, "Why do you keep looking back there?"

My spiritual eyes open, and suddenly I perceive that the windshield of my future is bigger than the rearview mirror of my past. That's where I will find hope again—ahead. Not behind.

Hmm. Is He right? Is my future bigger than the rearview mirror of my past? Is there hope still? Maybe He is right, and I just don't see it yet. My past seems to be chasing me, and I can't drive fast enough to get away from it.

This analogy has stuck with me, and over the years it has expanded and grown. Spend too much time looking into the rearview mirror, for example, and you will crash because you're not looking ahead. But never look back, and you may forget the wisdom of past seasons. There is also the reminder that, "Objects in the mirror may be closer than they appear." So, the mirror distorts the image, just like fear can distort things by making them appear more real than they are.

I have a favorite story from my driving times. Holy Spirit loves to poke at me when I get frustrated driving. It doesn't happen nearly as often as it used to, and I chalk that up to healing and getting older. I don't nearly as often give Holy Spirit the satisfaction of saying, "What's going on with you today?" as I respond, "They aren't using their turn signal." To which He will inevitably say, "Okay—so what's *really* going on?"

Ugh. He's always right—it's never really about the other drivers. I am usually impatient for some reason and I am taking it out on the other drivers. Even my BFF will now ask me what's going on with me if I get impatient in the car—even when I'm not driving.

This reminds me of "forgetting what lies behind and reaching forward." (This is from Philippians 3:13b NKJV, and has been a wildly-misused scripture in my world: a way of not dealing with the emotions of trauma and implying we should just forget past hurts.) How just like Holy Spirit to bring a scripture into my driving lessons.

We *glance* in that rearview mirror, yet we *look* out the windshield. We don't always remember what's back there, until we need to change lanes or stop quickly. We need to make sure we don't get hit from behind or side-swipe anyone, and that's why that mirror is there. But we just glance and make sure all is good. Then we look ahead and forget about what was back there as we forge on. We continue to glance back as we journey from place to place. But it's for safety, not because we live there.

Now here is the sticky part. If we can't at times forget what lies behind, it isn't truly behind us. Like the memory above that I kept reliving. It's riding shotgun in the car. This is where I think the hiccup is. That's the part that seems to get lost in this scripture when it's taught. I couldn't forget the memory I hadn't healed from.

So, what do you do in this case?

If it's not behind you, you keep taking it with you as you journey and it keeps getting unloaded and repacked in the car. How do you get it out of the passenger seat and leave it behind you?

You know when you're driving and you have to pee really badly, but you don't want to get off on an exit, but you also don't want to wet your car? What do you do? Where do you stop?

Yep, you stop at a rest area. You pull off, do your business, stretch your legs and then you keep going with that rest stop in the rearview mirror. You are probably feeling some relief. You've left what was causing you discomfort behind you. It's no longer "in the car" with you, so to speak. You remember needing to pee and the rest stop and you are thankful you didn't make a mess. But you are moving forward again. The rest area is in the rearview mirror, and you are now looking forward through the windshield.

What "going to the rest area" means for you may be just taking some time to rest, or to H.A.L.T. (to make sure you aren't **H**ungry, **A**ngry, **L**onely or **T**ired— see Chapter Six for more on this). It may also be time to seek some inner healing or simply phone a friend. Maybe get some prayer, take a hot bath, or get a counselor. I am not sure what is right for you. We are all different and unique. This is where self-awareness and the rearview mirror can be helpful to find clues as to what has helped us to leave the past behind us before, so that we can do that again now. Or, if something hasn't worked, take the time now to find something that does.

My thinking is, "I made it this far, so something along the way must have helped me to get to where I am in life. What were some of those things, and how can they help me again, now that I need a rest area?" Or, what hasn't worked that I am doing, and what new thing might I need to try? Maybe right now your rest area means stopping to ask yourself these questions and to explore inside yourself to find the answers.

LOOK OUT THE windshield

Remember This Principle When….

- You feel fearful.

- You feel like you can't settle and are anxious.

- You feel like you're going around in circles.

- You're struggling with patterns from the past that are holding you back.

CHAPTER 5

wayfinding

I don't think I am the only one who Holy Spirit likes to talk to when I'm driving. I suspect He does this with a lot of people. I don't know why for sure, but I think it's because our mind is engaged and we aren't filling it with "stuff."

One time as I was driving, I came to a multi-layered overpass, underpass, "around pass" interchange, the lanes twisted and intertwined like spaghetti. Holy Spirit says, "That's you and your relationships."

"What?" I responded, semi-annoyed—like that's supposed to make sense! I know He is goading me into asking questions, like my kid does when he wants attention.

He seemed to be focusing on all these lanes, all these cars passing, going different directions—each one with a person driving, and some with passengers.

Feeling a little thick at this point, again I said, "What?"

He went on to explain how each relationship has its own lane, because each one is unique. If I try to put different people into the same lane, they crash or clash, in most cases. Not everyone is going to be the same, so not everyone needs the same permissions. I can set different boundary lanes with different people. I don't have to put people in categories or stereotypes to get to know them as individuals or try to understand them. Not all relationships are the same and there doesn't need to be jealousy or comparison.

This analogy has unfolded and expanded to become a map with roads, road signs, and laws (and don't forget that the law is good).

In the natural, there is a whole transportation system with tests that you take to be permitted to drive and with a highway patrol. It's an entire ecosystem of its own that has been growing, expanding, and updating for centuries. Green, yellow, and red lights let us know when it's safe to go, when to slow down, and when you had better just stop all together. Each one of these visual pieces can have a parallel truth in the relational realm.

For example, when I was buying my house, I played a lot of "red light/green light." If something felt "off," or if a deal was being made that I wasn't comfortable with, I had permission to turn it in my mind to a red light or a yellow light. That would then give me a green light to look into another house option.

Sometimes I had to "yield" to another offer, or sometimes I had to yield by deciding not to hit the road that day, because I needed time to decompress and reevaluate.

By thinking through the process in this way, by comparing it with something I already logically understood the meaning of, I was able to process through it without getting overly emotional and making emotional decisions. I wasn't easily pressured. It gave me words for what I was feeling and the ability to explain it to others in a more universal language.

Lanes

So, let's go back to the super-highway and lanes. Lanes are like boundaries—all relationships need them and all relationships have them, even if they aren't spoken. The danger comes in dealing with people who don't have boundaries. They will inevitably have trouble with yours.

I've learned to watch out for people who are always changing lanes relationally, weaving in and out of traffic, especially with no turn signal. Like driving, it's okay if someone is going in a different direction, and it's okay if they aren't in the same lane. But let's be careful to not whip a U-turn at high speeds and try to go in a different direction relationally. There is a safe, easy and legal way to make a U-turn with patience and fewer consequences—like someone getting hurt.

An example of this in real life may be when you are starting a new job. We've all been there. It takes time to learn your place—to learn the job, the people, the rhythm. You may get your toes stepped on and you may step on toes—those are the boundaries or lanes. So we adjust, we align, and we learn that things may not be as we thought initially. But if we can see it like a road map, we can apply those signs and lessons to it.

We can take a look and see if we need to slow down, for example. Maybe we have too much zeal and it's causing us to speed and not consider the danger we are putting others in. We may need to see how this transportation system works before we try to change everything, or think that we know it all. Maybe it's a red light and this isn't where we belong. Or, maybe it's a green light to suggest some things that may streamline the process. Maybe we just need to yield to the policies and procedures already in place and humble ourselves.

Signage

Visually there are signs, roadmaps, billboards, etc., all giving us information to make the drive more safe and enjoyable. Then when we get where we are going, there are usually what we call wayfinding signs, which just means signs to help us find our way.

In a past job, I used to work for a sign company where I learned the importance of ADA (Americans with Disabilities Act) signs and wayfinding signs.

Before this job, I hadn't considered what it would be like to go somewhere, like a hospital, and not have any signs telling you where to go, where to park, or where the bathrooms and elevators were. It would be frustrating and could cause a lot of anxiety.

Holy Spirit had a hey-day with this new information I'd learned.

I was coordinating an event, and my boss was pulling a "Do as I say, not as I do" stunt. I was trying to keep the event on budget. But he would go and spend a bunch of money on things that went over the allotted funds. This left my budget out of balance—and me along with it.

Holy Spirit asked if I knew why this was making me so anxious.

"You know me better than I know myself and You don't know the answer to that?" I asked. "Yes, I am anxious."

"Do you know why you are anxious?" He asked again.

I said, "He's my boss, he's this, he's that. *Yada yada yada.*"

To which Holy Spirit replied, "No, there's no signage."

Which left me saying, "Huh?"

He explained that signage is a way of communicating. If there are no signs, there is no communication, which makes people anxious because they don't know where to go or what to do.

Well, wasn't that just a kick in the teeth? I finally got the message. I needed to create some wayfinding signs for my boss. I needed to clean up my side of the street and clarify, with signage, the boundaries of the budget.

So, I went to my boss and explained the budget and how I had a bonus riding on it. I showed him how it was getting off-balance and how we wouldn't be able to do what he wanted because of the overspending. I also let him know that was going to reflect negatively on me, him *and* the event I was hired to coordinate.

Did he stick to the budget? Nope. I, however, was less anxious. I had done what I could and had communicated clearly, which left him to make his own choice. (And yes, I did get the bonus in the end, for those who need the end to the story).

I'll wrap up with this: we are not always going to be perfect or be able to follow every road sign. That's what grace is for, along with mercy and forgiveness.

When lanes are getting crossed, or you aren't sure about them, or turn signals aren't being used, it may be time to hit a rest area. Perhaps, you may realize that something is a yellow light or that it may be time to yield.

Remember the windshield and the rearview mirror? All that has been written on your map is in your rearview mirror of learning. You still have the open windshield ahead. You still have that unwritten part of the map to draw and to live into.

Sometimes, when cleaning up our side of the street, we may see the things from the past starting to repeat themselves. It may be telling us it's time to start looking at what signage we need to find our way again. We may realize the boundary lanes aren't clear, and communication and wayfinding signs are needed to clarify what's going on. Like cleaning up our side of the street, we can't wait for someone else to write our map for us. There is nothing wrong with taking the time at the rest area to be self-aware of what's going on with us personally. The rest stop of grace can be just the relief we need.

My hope is that this will make the road-not-yet-traveled a little easier for you to navigate, as you live into your own map for the future.

Remember This Principle When....

- You're having trouble navigating relationships.

- You want to communicate clearly.

- You are making a big decision.

- You're starting a new endeavor.

CHAPTER 6

OXYGEN *mask*

I have done everything I know to do:
Bottle. *Check.*
Clean diaper. *Check.*
Walk in the stroller. *Check.*
Baby Swing. *Check.*
Play time. *Check.*
Called Nana for help. *Check.*
Nap. *Check.*

So why are you still screaming at me? What did I do wrong? Where is your father? He should have been home by now!

Piles of laundry and dishes also scream for my attention. *The house smells like I forgot to take the diaper to the trash. The yard needs to be mowed. What are we having for dinner?*

"Here, it's your turn!" I scream, handing my son, who is just a few months old, to his father as he finally walks in the door.

I am stressing. Our "home study" case manager could stop by anytime to do a "pop-up" visit that still needs to be completed before she can sign off that we are appropriate as parents for our adopted son.

Put on Your Oxygen Mask First

Have you ever been on an airplane, listening to the flight attendant give the announcements? They explain how the oxygen mask will drop down from above if needed, and emphasize that you should put yours on first, before helping anyone else. Do you know *why* we are told to put our mask on first? Because you can't help anyone if you are dead!

I know, it seems obvious, but it's amazing how we can forget that principle when moving through day-to-day life.

In those first few months with us, our son barely slept. He had tummy issues that we were working with his doctor to resolve. For what seemed like an eternity, he cried and cried every time he ate. And I cried because I felt helpless and like a terrible mom. It was a mess. I felt like *we* were a mess. I lived with the constant fear hanging over my head that a pop-up visit would catch me in the middle of this kind of chaos and I would be found to be an unfit parent.

After that moment of exhaustion, melt down and screaming at my son's father—oh my goodness! I learned really quick to nap when my son napped. If I wasn't rested and patient, either he would be fussier, or I wouldn't be able to calm him because *I* wasn't able to be calm. So, I decided that the house could stay a mess. I needed to take a nap to take care of myself, in order to take care of him. He needed to be more important than the state of the house.

This principle goes back to that scripture that says, "Love your neighbor as yourself" (Matthew 19:19). How are you going to save your neighbor if you can't breathe? When we get *our* oxygen mask on, we realize the damage that our inability to breathe has had on those we love, because they suffer also.

I had another realization of this in my first two years of sobriety. I had started to have some painful memories pop up. After some thought, I decided to step down from the inner healing I was teaching, because I realized I had some inner healing to do myself.

As the healing went deeper, I then made the decision to pull back from some relationships with people who were trying to tell me what my reality was. I needed to find out for myself what was real and what wasn't. In other words, I needed to get *my* oxygen mask on and heal, before I would be ready to help other people heal from what they thought was true. This was also when I started building my "bubble" of a safe space. I explain this more in *Creating a Bubble,* Chapter Ten.

I'll be the first to admit that I thought that if I helped others, it would also help me. But when I got burned out, I realized that *I* was the one who needed help. I saw that helping others wasn't helping me. Instead, my life was falling apart, as those I was helping were doing better.

H.A.L.T.

One day, a woman called me who I knew had been going through a tough situation. She was about to take her son to the hospital for a mental health evaluation. She was very emotional, but she knew she needed to be strong, stable and at peace for her son. So, I said to her, "Halt."

"First off," I asked her, "Have you eaten today?"

She hadn't, so I said, "Go get a meal that is healthy and high in protein. Then get off your phone and just sit in the restaurant and eat. Call me back when you're done."

In the span of time it took for her to order food, eat and call me, she had become a different person. By feeding her body, she was centering herself on her most immediate need. And, rather than listening to anyone else or rehashing what was happening, she had focused on her need instead of what everyone else thought, and she was now ready to face whatever was ahead.

A good way to assess the basics of whether your oxygen mask is on or not is "H.A.L.T.," which is what I was actually telling her to do.

H.A.L.T. means **H**ungry, **A**ngry, **L**onely or **T**ired. H.A.L.T. is a way to learn when we are most vulnerable—or when our oxygen mask isn't on. These four basic things (hungry, angry, lonely and tired) are clear indicators to stop and do a self-evaluation: are we helping everyone else put their oxygen mask on without getting ours on first?

For example, are you eating? Nutrition is a practical way to help us get the "oxygen" our body needs and to care for ourselves. This includes not only *whether* we eat, but also *what* we eat. I'm definitely not here to judge what you are eating. I used to go from work to college classes and I would often forget to eat during my day. I would grab a bag of chips from a vending machine when a nurse told me not to forget the chocolate bar because it would sustain my energy and cause me not to crash as quickly. What "nutrition" is for you is your business. Just make sure you're taking care of yourself so you're not **H**ungry.

The A is for **A**ngry. If you are angry a lot or impatient, more times than not the anger is there to cover over pain. It's an indication to look within. This might also be a sign of some grieving that needs to take place where we are avoiding the pain. The stages of grief are real. (A little side note: times of transition often have some pain, loss or grief attached, even good transitions.)

In addition, I learned that we can feel **Lonely**, even when there are people around. This might be because we have put walls up in order to survive. This would be a clue to help you realize you may be in a place where you need to find someone else who has their oxygen mask on and ask them for help.

Or, are you always **Tired**, feeling weak, drained or unmotivated? Are you sleeping well? Have you taken on too much? Any of these indicators can help you realize that you may be trying to love others without loving yourself first.

It is so very important to learn what self-care is for you. What gives *you* oxygen? What breathes in life for you? Where do you need to take care of you, first? And let's just throw a monkey wrench in here. Start by asking yourself the question, "Do I care about myself?"

That was a huge revelation when I asked myself that. I realized I knew how to care *for* myself, but did I care *about* myself? This went from not just doing nice things for myself, but doing them *because* I love who I am as a person. Do I care about myself in the same way I want others to care about me? Do I care about how I feel and how I am doing? Instead of waiting for others to check in on you, are you checking in on yourself?

Now as I usually do, I am going to add the caveat that caring for yourself is not permission to put people off forever or to go into hibernation or to not do anything for anyone else. I am assuming that, if you are reading this, you are an adult and know that you can't stop working if you need income, for example. So, this isn't permission to "take care of yourself" by quitting a job so that you can help yourself first. That isn't actually going to accomplish what I am talking about. We aren't looking for a pendulum swing here, but rather how you can daily or weekly better care for yourself. If you are in a situation where you may need to change some things more drastically, ask for help from someone who has their oxygen mask on. It is perfectly fine to realize you need help. We all need people.

Some people I've helped over the years simply needed to stop during the day and take their lunch break, instead of pressing through because they were trying to get things done. For others, it might be to actually take the weekend to do weekend things so you can go back to work more rested and able to accomplish more. If you have a lot of drama around you and need to create internal peace, creating the "bubble" (Chapter Ten) may be what you need.

The key though, is this: self-evaluation. Self-evaluation can let you know where you are and what you need. When we care about ourselves and self-evaluate, we can make a plan to focus on making time to have our needs met in a healthy way. I also recommend to not do self-evaluation alone all of the time, so that negative self-talk doesn't rule the conversation.

Even Jesus stole away and took time for Himself. So why do we chastise ourselves for needing that same thing, or call it selfish?

Not only that, if I can't breathe, what am I teaching my son? How well am I helping those I coach if I am giving them the bottom of the barrel all the time? Or—and this isn't a joke—if I start to lose my filter and jump on their bandwagon, or climb on my soap box, or rant because I am tired, crabby and down-right just don't care. Now that is *selfish*, not self-care.

So, back to my earlier questions: what helps you put on your oxygen mask? It can be different for everyone. Maybe it's pursuing a hobby, music, reading, writing, or making time for friends. Perhaps you may want to find a coach. Maybe it's been a while and you will need to ask a friend to help you see what you need. What are some things that you're passionate about that you haven't done in a while?

A friend used to ask me, "What is a hobby of yours?" I had no idea. I had to take time to think about what I like to do and start doing that again. I also learned to try new things to find out if there was a hobby I hadn't tapped into yet.

For me, loving myself can be as simple as making a hot cup of tea during a busy day. I like to cook, so sometimes I might just cook a nice meal for no reason. Sometimes, what I need is to plan an overnight vacation, or give myself permission to not make plans for a few days and have a "staycation." My kid needs these too. At other times, I even go so far as to say to myself, "I am going to do what I do when I am sick, in order to prevent myself from getting sick." So, I order take-out and watch TV or read.

Helping Your Neighbor

Okay, so now we can finally get to the other half of the equation—helping someone else put their oxygen mask on. The "loving your neighbor" part.

Assuming we now have our mask securely on and we are getting the oxygen we need, it's time for phase two. Not everyone will receive oxygen in the same way. However, since we have our mask on, we know how to lead them to what helps them breathe, without telling them to do it our way. (That wouldn't be oxygen, that would be suffocation.)

I have learned through the years to pay attention to those I love, in order to learn how I can love them and help them breathe.

I am a little "extra," so I usually end up smothering them in attention, but I am getting better. My Bestie loves red roses. Once, I got like 50 of them for her. Realizing that may have been a little overkill, I now stick with two dozen.

Sometimes, helping someone put their oxygen mask on means doing something for them that they wouldn't do for themselves, in the way that *they* receive love. This is the part that isn't about us; it's about them. This is also learning intimacy, to really see others. Maybe they need to H.A.L.T. and need help working that out. For example, my kid gets "hangry," so I always keep snacks on hand, just in case.

What this all boils down to is love: both for others and for us. What if we turned the scripture about loving our neighbors as ourselves into a question: "How well do I love myself? Is my self-talk uplifting? Would I speak to anyone else in the way I do to myself, and would it be considered loving?"

I can guarantee that if you don't love yourself the way you *think* you are, loving others won't really be love. It will more likely be manipulation, control, or co-dependency. If we are trying to help others in order to make ourselves feel good, is that really love, or is it an expectation? We can't make everyone happy, we can't make others love us, and we can't help everyone. That isn't realistic, and that's okay.

What we *can* do is love ourselves and let that love spill over to others.

OXYGEN
mask

Remember This Principle When….

- You realize you're helping others more than yourself.

- You are hungry, angry, lonely or tired (H.A.L.T).

- You are overwhelmed.

- You feel burned out or short-tempered.

CHAPTER 7

pain TOLERANCE

The cool air of a slight breeze touches my face as I walk the beach. The sun is shining, the water warm. Suntan lotion is the aromatic accompaniment to Jax Beach on any summer day. I enjoy the sound of kids squealing in delight—at least, I do until I realize that one of those squeals isn't delight.

"My ball, my ball!" he's pointing out at the ocean, where the tide is carrying his ball away.

"I'll get it," I offer, running after it.

BAM! I run smack dab into a rock just under the surface of the water, catching it with my big toe. OUCH!

I still manage to save the ball, hand it to the kid and spend some time explaining to his family about the tide. Out-of-towners just don't get it.

Well, that was fun. Except now it's a two-mile walk back to my car.

Womp! Womp! Womp! throbs my toe with every step. *Breathe. Breathe. You got this. Almost there—just one more mile.*

"Oh crap!" I whisper, looking up at the steps I still need to climb to get back to the parking lot where my car is. "I don't got *this*!"

And just at that moment, an angel—I'm sure—in the form of a woman, scoops me up under my arms and assists me up the stairs. Relief washes over me.

Somehow, I get myself home, even with the excruciating pain. By nightfall, my toe is swollen and turning colors. By the next morning, it's become huge. My skin is splitting, swollen like a sausage about to bust open. No way I can go to the gym today. I turn to my best friends, ice, Tylenol and Advil, and take it easy.

The next day, I assess the pain level of my black-and-blue toe against the possible pain level of starting smoking again—the only two options I can see at the time. I wrap my toe in five layers of gauze and squeeze my foot into my tennis shoes. I head to the gym. Going to the gym helps me to not smoke, and I can't start again now.

Goodbye, Alligator Skin

I'm telling you this story because, over the past several years, I have prayed a prayer that, honestly, I'm not sure was my best idea ever. Had it not seemed prompted by Holy Spirit, I am not sure I would have prayed it.

It started years earlier while sitting in my office. My son was young and we had been reading a book about an alligator. I don't remember the book, but I remember Holy Spirit talking to me about the alligator's skin. About how alligator skin is thick, rough and there to protect the alligator. And, how I wore the same thing.

What I understood from this conversation with Holy Spirit was that He was showing me how I keep my walls up and have a protective skin so that I don't get hurt. I also understood that I do this so that others won't see just how much I hurt. I project an "I got this" attitude. But I had to ask myself, in reality, do I really "got this"?

Fast-forward more than a year from the timing of this alligator skin conversation. I had a vision while I was driving. (I still have no idea how these things happen and I don't crash. Only the supernatural can explain this, because I sure as heck can't!)

In the vision, I was on a stage in an auditorium with a huge spotlight pointed on me. The room was full of people. I felt so vulnerable and transparent (not unlike how I feel in writing this book), like everyone could see my every flaw. Yet, strangely, I was unashamed. I looked down and there was a bullet-proof vest—like that alligator skin—laying on the stage next to me. I was just standing there, in my true self, being seen. Then I heard a line from a song about being the wind beneath someone's wings. I realized that the real "me" is my wind beneath my wings. Under all those walls of protection, the real me was now shining bright in that spotlight. I had nothing to be ashamed of.

So, what is this oh-so-powerful prayer I began praying from that first moment in my office after reading the alligator book? And that I have continued to pray since having that vision of the stage?

"God, lower my pain tolerance." So simple, yet so profound.

The result of this prayer is usually a whole lot of tears, layer upon layer of repentance, crying at the drop of a hat, inexplicable pain rising to the surface, and a lot of me asking for forgiveness. But I also soften, and a restfulness comes deep into my being. I feel more sheltered, more protected, more cared for. The irony is that this happens *even though* I have let down the guardedness that I thought was actually doing all this for me. It becomes clear that my guardedness was not what was protecting me—it was just increasing the pain on the inside.

Another result of this prayer is that I will see deeper layers to the people and places that have wounded me. I see the pain that I still carry that isn't mine to carry, because it's not "my side of the street." I give myself permission to forgive and to resolve the matter in my heart. Once I find acceptance in my mind, I don't have to carry all that pain with me. I can leave it at the rest stop. I can't change what happened to cause the pain, but I can change how I look at it and how I heal. I do have a choice.

In addition, as a result of this prayer, I become more aware of the times, places and relationships when I used pain as a measure of what I could or couldn't handle. I would ask myself, "If this were to go badly, is my skin thick enough to take another hit?"

I've used this question even to assess the amount of physical pain I think I can handle. Three weeks after the toe incident I just described, I was still going to the gym and experiencing excruciating pain. I finally went to the doctor to have my toe examined. He ordered x-rays, which revealed that my toe was fractured. The doctor's response was, "Yeah, so this is real—you have been walking around with an avulsion fracture for the last three weeks. No, it isn't your imagination—you are definitely hurt."

Fast-forward three months later, I'm still going to the gym and I've now been told I will have to have surgery on my toe—because I still hadn't stopped my pace. The doctor finally told me that my pain tolerance was high. He said I had gotten so used to the pain that I didn't realize that the fractured bone in the joint and its tendon had all fully separated. It all needed to be screwed back together. (For those of you wondering, no, I haven't gone back to smoking, and yes, I had surgery and got it all put back together.)

Tough Doesn't Mean Holy

Realizing the consequences that shoving my foot into that sneaker and going to the gym had had, in addition to the pain, led me back, yet again, to the prayer, "God, lower my pain tolerance!" Why do I think I have to be so tough? Do I think I have something to prove?

Somewhere along the way, we are taught that pressing through pain is somehow holy, righteous—even celebrated. But being tough isn't a badge of honor. Neither is suffering in silence—following that old adage of *don't talk, don't trust, don't feel*. We point to all of our wounds and say, "Hey, look at everything I've been through and *I* am still going!" Or, we seek pity, which also increases pain. So the result of this false belief that pressing through pain is "holy" can be either a prideful mentality or a victim mentality—you choose.

When all these thoughts and feelings get twisted into allowing pain to take up residence in us (rather than processing through the pain), we won't acknowledge the hurts and wrongs done to us, nor will we acknowledge the hurts we've caused. These tendencies keep us from forgiveness—the very freedom the pain needs in order to heal.

When we ignore the hurt and our need for forgiveness, we then begin to reject ourselves and others, in the process of rejecting pain. Reject it long enough, and rejection or being rejected becomes our norm—to the point that, if something actually healthy comes along, we can't even recognize it!

When we put on that bullet-proof vest or the alligator skin, no one can come close and no one can hurt us. Everything becomes surface interactions. So, we live our life without ever truly knowing ourselves or anyone else. We can even begin to search for relationship-replacers to fulfill the desire of our heart to be known, heard, seen, and loved. I'll talk more about this in a minute.

Not forgiving or asking for forgiveness when we have wronged ourselves or someone else is like carrying around a whole bunch of debt we can never work hard enough or enough hours to repay. We end up constantly in the red. Being in the red should serve to alert us that it may be time to look for a "rest area" on our journey and re-evaluate.

How many times have I said, "You've got this" or "I've got this" and then forged on ahead—when what I really needed was to have a good cry or to allow someone else to just vent, cry and feel? We tell ourselves (or we are told) what we should do, could do, need to do, even *have* to do instead of letting it out—the hurt, the pain, the shame, the condemnation, or the confession.

What we can do is break down the wall, take off the thick skin, and shelter our hearts in a place that feels safe and protected, like home. We may need to allow ourselves to just cry it out, to admit the pain, to release it, to see where forgiveness needs to take place in order to allow a turn-around to happen.

As the saying goes, "Hurt people hurt people," and this is that cycle. How do we do our part to make it stop and address our own hurts? To start to heal from the inside out?

"God, lower my pain tolerance."

Relationship-replacers

So, this journey led me to these two questions:

Are the desires of my heart being clouded by pain? And does pain retract the heart?

High pain tolerance doesn't just cloud the truth of how much pain we are in, allowing more pain to build up, it also blocks our joy receptors. It blocks and can muddy the water of our dreams, hopes, and desires—the things that bring joy, love, and kindness. We don't just block out the bad; we block out the good.

So, think about this: as we block both pain and joy, we become numb. Like the Hoover Dam holds back water, a high wall of pain tolerance holds back the water of emotion. Without emotion, we can hurt people and not know it, because we're blocking both positive and negative emotions. We'll snap at people, criticize ourselves, not communicate or ignore people. We'll get close, and then as we begin to feel, we'll back off. We'll lack the capacity for intimacy that is so beautiful and brings joy to life. We can block out the very connections we so long for.

As the wall gets higher to hold back the pain, the water level of pain gets higher. The more we try to increase that wall, the more the water rises, the more pressure builds, the more pain from the pressure comes, and on and on goes the cycle.

As the pain tolerance increases, the need to feel increases. We can then go searching for things to help us feel better as "relationship replacers." We end up seeking things to make us feel better, such as buying things, or using drugs or alcohol—anything that we can use as a distraction to help us escape from negative feelings, or the lack of feeling.

Did you know that anger can be an addiction? That causing drama can be an addiction? Anything we become addicted to, whether it's a substance or not, is a relationship-replacer.

These behaviors numb the pain and cause us to focus on something or someone else or to create blame for how we are feeling. When we don't deal with and acknowledge our own pain, we don't see and acknowledge anyone else's. We tolerate abusive behavior—or our own abusive behavior—and this becomes normal. I am not saying that we can't have discernment or that we should wear rose-colored glasses. *Healthy* boundaries are good to have. What I am addressing is that filtering everything through unresolved pain causes more pain. In this cycle, joy, dreams, healing, and our heart itself all retract.

As we hide our hearts behind this wall of unprocessed pain, we block out love and begin to fear kindness. Even gentleness begins to hurt, because harshness and pain are normal. Wires get crossed and the meaning of things changes. It becomes harder and harder to define what things like "gentleness" and "compassion" even are. Even one small, random act of kindness can bring our whole wall crashing down, and we'll find ourselves sobbing or feeling undeserving—maybe even questioning the motives of the kindness or responding in unhealthy ways. We may finally become unable to recognize what kindness is.

As we begin to walk out our dreams, as we seek love, as we try something new, as we open ourselves to a new relationship or to rekindle or repair an existing one, all of that old hurt and pain will eventually resurface. We will then be faced with choices. We can choose to either allow the pain to continue—to drop the ball on the dream and avoid pain again—or, we can choose to lower our pain tolerance, heal and stop the cycle.

Too often, we decide to put that alligator skin back on in order to feel bullet-proof as we allow the bullets of pain to fly—not realizing how much pain we are adding to ourselves and those around us in the process. Our thinking can become, "If I can get over it, so can they." Thus, the wake of broken relationships and lost hopes and dreams will continue to increase.

But, if we will choose to stand on that stage—spotlight on us, vulnerable, transparent and unencumbered—we will show the world what is possible when we take the wall down and allow ourselves to be seen and heard, to have a face and a name. We will allow the true strength that comes from within our healed heart to grow. We will begin to see and hear those around us, and will turn the cycle of hurt into a cycle of healing. Healing people heal people.

We can begin to live where pain and healing can be simultaneous as we walk through it and refuse to get stuck. We will spend more time living out our hopes and dreams. We will experience love instead of fear, rejection, hurt, pain and unforgiveness.

There's a saying I learned early on in recovery: "We can't change other people, we can only change ourselves. Other people will change in reaction to our change."

We can't wait for others to change to start healing our hurts and pains. We can't wait for other people to change to realize our dreams, to have hopes, to heal relationships or to start new ones. The only one who can choose to heal our pain and live in freedom is ourselves.

And it starts with: "God, lower my pain tolerance."

pain TOLERANCE

Remember This Principle When….

- You realize you may be pushing people away.

- You are feeling the need to guard or protect yourself.

- You are looking for ways out of dealing with your feelings: alcohol, drugs, sex, entertainment, etc.

- You find yourself isolating.

CHAPTER 8

redefine

At the beginning of each new year, I ask Holy Spirit for a word that will be helpful to me during the coming year.

In 2020, my word for the year was "revolution." *Hmmm....* Off I went to research the word.

"Noun: an overthrow or repudiation and the thorough replacement of an established government or political system by the people governed," Dictionary.com tells me.

Movies like *Hunger Games*, *Divergent*, and *V for Vendetta* pop into my head. The kind where the powers-that-be are overthrown by someone they underestimated.

Who am I to be a part of something so large? I wonder.

With this new word for the year at the forefront of my mind, I begin to hear it in songs and see it on commercials—signs from Holy Spirit letting me know, "You heard the right word, but keep digging."

I feel my insecurities rising to the surface—it's such a big word. So, I try to change it.

Re-reading my journal, I try to remind myself why this really is the word for the year—while also hoping I'll hear something different.

Nope. I still sense that's definitely the word. *Oh great, now what?* I think to myself.

Fast-forward a few months into 2020. I am still aware of the word and I accept that it's my word for the year, but I know that either I'm not really letting it sink in, or I'm not getting it.

I ask others, "What does revolution mean to you?" And I chew and chew and chew on the different perspectives, yet none of them really seem to fit either.

What if it means something different? I finally begin to ask myself.

No lie—by this point I'm starting to think maybe this is the word for 2021 or 2022 instead. Time isn't the same to an infinite God as it is to us. But He clearly responds, "No, time *isn't* the same to Me, but in your humanity, I created time in segments."

Okay, I get that, and my humanity really appreciates it. What else can I say?

I'm stumped, so I ask my seven-year-old son, because he makes everything so simple. "Buggie (that's his nickname), what does the word 'revolution' mean to you?"

"Duh, Mom—the sun going around the earth."

Insert palm to the face emoji here!

So back I go to the dictionary with a different perspective: "A single orbit of one object around another or about an axis or center. The Earth takes 365 days to make a revolution around the sun."

Bam! That's it! Now my spirit makes the connection with the word.

To which Holy Spirit says, "I love your process. I could have told you that's what I meant a long time ago, if you had just asked Me." Meanwhile, it seems to me like all of heaven is erupting in joyful laughter. Oh, how He loves my deep and wide processing and blind determination!

I wasn't super happy that it took me months to realize a real meaning of the word that I could land on—but at least it didn't take 365 days!

So, for the rest of that year, "revolution" came to remind me of a principle.

God set the universe and solar system in motion with beauty and precision, so that the earth travels around the sun without the earth doing anything other than being itself.

Similarly, what God sets in motion in my life in a year happens in the same way. I will revolve around the Son, 365 days a year, by being myself.

We Don't Know What We Don't Know

This whole experience made me aware that sometimes, we will define something a certain way, yet it can mean something far different, depending on who you are and your experiences. "Love," "faith," "spirit," "mean," "nice," "kind"—all of these things can have different meanings at different times and for different people. A meaning can also shift throughout a person's life span.

A couple years ago, I read this book called *Think Again* by Adam Grant. If, like me, you are a deep and wide processor in your thinking, this book may help you to celebrate that. If you aren't, this book may help you see why thinking differently is an asset.

My take-away, in lay terms, is in this example:

Reach way back in your memory to those early grade school years—remember those science projects we all did? Science projects were about allowing yourself to approach things with a hypothesis and to gather evidence *before* drawing a conclusion. The projects taught us to keep an open mind, because we don't know what we don't know.

Now, consider scientific industries like NASA, where people are always learning, exploring, and pushing the limits—because they are always willing to think again. Imagine those same grade school kids now working at NASA. Imagine that their science project never actually stopped. They had a hypothesis and they continued to gather evidence. They proved one hypothesis, and it led them to the next and the next.

What this means is that a conclusion is actually the *beginning* of the next hypothesis. They evolve.

When we stop being willing to keep an open mind, to redefine something, we camp out on a definition of something that may actually need to expand. Like *Staying on The Side of Truth* explains, if we camp out on what is "true," we won't look for "truth," nor expand all the way to the higher truth, "Divine Truth."

When we don't allow room for redefinition, we can get stuck. We can allow everything we hear to get filtered through a definition that hasn't yet expanded. Take, for example, our definition of love. If what we define love to be is based on conditions, then anything without those conditions we will not define as love. Or, to some people, peace is actually drama. To others peace might be isolation.

It may be time to look at some of our definitions and allow redefinition to come into them. Maybe you thought you'd be further along in life than you are right now. It's likely time to redefine that, instead of being defeated by it. See where you currently are as a starting point to your new life, rather than an end to the life you thought you would have. Redefine. Allow Holy Spirit to redefine your identity in this new place. I am not saying there won't be loss or grief, but I *am* saying there is hope.

Perhaps you're facing some kind of transition with your kids or your parents. Times and seasons change, and a redefinition can come along with it. Maybe the conclusion you arrived at years ago fit where you were then, but it no longer fits where you are now. It may not be sufficient to take you as far as you are going to go. As healing takes place, redefining accompanies it. Keep redefining.

redefine

Remember This Principle When….

- You begin to wonder if something really means what you think it means.

- You find yourself in transition.

- You are doing what you've always done, but it's no longer working.

- When something used to "click" for you, but it no longer does.

CHAPTER 9

the WINNING HAND

Sometimes, when I am just sitting at home, doing something mindless in an attempt to rest and detox from a busy week, Holy Spirit thinks it's funny to whisper a thought that reverberates through my whole being. Something that suddenly shifts me from mindlessness to deep pondering. I am not sure why He has the gall to interrupt my mindless plan, other than it works every time (insert eye roll and a sarcastic half smile emojis here).

That may sound ungrateful, but I'm not. Holy Spirit and I just get a little punchy at times and tease each other. I'd like to think it's because we are friends, so I feel more myself when this kind of thing happens.

So, one night, I was sitting there just minding my own business, when He oh-so-quietly whispers to me, "You know that hand you're holding close to your chest—that winning hand? It's best to give it to Me if you want your cards played right."

Now, in case that sounds really weird, let me give the CliffsNotesversion backstory on why this was such a reverberating moment for me.

A few years back, I went through a hard time that changed my life drastically. When hard things come along, my response is to journal through it. I write out all the feelings, thoughts, anger, judgements, challenges and my responses to them—all of it. It's like a form of meditation for me. It helps me to get all the stuff out of my mind and heart so that I can gain a different perspective, but without all the noise. It is also a way I can express myself without the pain of regret that "going off on someone" in the heat of the moment may cause. It also opens me up to hear from others and Jesus—once I have dumped my stuff and quieted my soul.

In this particular instance, after I got all the ranting down on paper, the Holy Spirit walked me through a daydream of sorts. It then continued to unfold for a few days, following the initial experience.

In this time of journaling my "holy imagination," I was at a casino, sitting at a high-stakes poker table. I was in one seat playing, beside me was a dealer, and all the other seats were full—which meant I wasn't the only one playing. The pot in the middle was so huge that chips were avalanching off the chip mountain. I had cards in my hand and I was waiting to see what I would catch "in the river."

It was loud; all the players were commenting and trying to intimidate the other players. And I *felt* intimidated: by the players, the dealer, the high stakes, the atmosphere, and my own thoughts.

The biggest thought intimidating me was, "I don't belong here." I am a risk-taker by nature, but I'm also calculated, and I knew I didn't have the money to back the chips on the table. If I lost, I would lose big and I would stay lost for a long time before I could recover from gambling away that much money.

It was then that the song *The Gambler* by Kenny Rogers came to my mind. I'm sure the lyrics are running through your head right now.

So I had to look up the song, as I know for me, songs usually have more meaning than I realize at first.

I was glad that I did, because when I'd heard the song in my head, in the line about counting one's money, I thought I'd heard it say not to count your *blessings*, rather than money. And then I thought the next line said, "when the deal is done," rather than "dealing." (You can look the lyrics up yourself, because if I quoted them here, I'd have to go through the potentially costly process of getting permission to do so.)

A High Stakes Game

Anyway, it was at this point that I realized that every chip on the table in my daydream didn't represent money—instead, each one was a blessing in place of a curse that the enemy of negativity was throwing down against me. One chip was "Failure," one "Rebellious," another "Unlovable," and so on. But on the other side of each chip was the opposite: "Accepted," "Successful," "Unstoppable," "Courageous," and so forth. This really *was* a high stakes game!

As in most of my holy imagination journaling, I couldn't see what the cards I had were, so I didn't know if it was a good hand. (I sometimes can get a sense of something, but I rarely see numbers or words in these excursions with Holy Spirit.) Knowing Holy Spirit is always with me, I started drilling Him with questions. He never really answers me until I get to the place of less shooting-in-the-dark questions and start to ask the questions that really matter.

I have also learned in these Spirit times to say to myself, "Clear the mechanism." (Yes, this is from the movie *For Love of the Game*.) It's a verbal reminder to clear away all the noise and confusion originally present and to focus in on the main thing happening, removing the distraction. (We do not lose free will in any type of dreaming.) So, I put all the noise on mute so that my sense of sight was able to increase and focus. Who was I playing against? What was in the pot that I was betting on? How good was my hand? This is the calculated-risk part.

Holy Spirit let me know, while journaling what was happening in my imagination, that this wasn't a new game; it's been around a long time. I was playing against the enemy of my soul, and I was playing for my freedom from the lies I still believed. He also said to hold the cards close to my chest and to remain silent. He explained that there would be a perfect time to play my cards, and that I held the winning hand.

I wanted to know why I couldn't just play my hand, get it over with and go about the business of counting my blessings (which is what I thought the song lyric said). He let me know that the more the enemy threw into the pot, the higher my winnings would be. Since I had the winning hand already, I should just let them throw in everything they had and make all the noise they wanted. It did nothing other than give me more. For everything they threw in, I also threw in what I thought I didn't have, which gave me a higher return and kept the game going by raising the stakes. Holy Spirit showed me that He was the one dealing the hands, and that the other players didn't think I could win against them. But unbeknownst to them, their hands were powerless against mine.

Over the years since this took place, I have held onto the truths and experience of this journal session. It has strengthened me, helped me stay on the side of truth and increased my trust and faith along the way.

I even bought a deck of cards and pinned the ultimate winning poker hand to a cork board as a reminder.

I will be honest, there have been times when I have whined to Holy Spirit, God, and Jesus about how their timing sucks—mostly when the assaults of the "negativity" enemy seem greater than my ability to endure. I have wanted to throw my cards face down on the table and walk away, tired of the game. I have wanted to pridefully yell at them and tell them I have the winning hand, so they better back off. Every time, He is faithfully gentle and rejuvenates me.

So, let's return to the present day and how this was a "redefining" moment for me. As I mentioned, I was sitting there, minding my own business, when Holy Spirit said, "You know that hand you're holding close to your chest—that winning hand? It's best to give it to Me if you want your cards played right."

This hand is the thing I have held onto for hope for my future. It had become my weapon of peace, strength, truth, and encouragement—a place of safety and courage. I trusted this hand to get me through hard times. More accurately, I trusted the words given me by my Beloved about this hand, the pot in the middle, the whole story that played out in my imagination. I believed it meant that I would win against the onslaught of negativity and couldn't lose.

And yet now—He wanted me to give it back to Him? The hand He gave me that had gotten me this far, the tool that helped shape my journey—He now wanted it back?

"But why?" I asked. "Didn't You tell me to hang onto it and to play at the perfect moment?"

What came next wasn't the most pleasant of moments.

Holy Spirit so kindly, yet in a very deliberate way, let me know that yes, it would be played at the perfect moment—but *not if I kept holding onto it*.

"Well then, why'd You give it to me in the first place, if You were just going to take it back?" I demanded.

Needless to say, I wasn't happy with where this conversation was going. I wrestled back and forth with this for days, then again turned to my journal, where the revelation came.

Sovereignty and Control

I had the hand, I held it close, I stayed safe and quiet in the onslaught *because I also held onto the notion that I could control when the hand was played.* **I** held the power. I'd had times when I wanted to play it before and went to Him on timing. But even then, I still held the power of controlling the timing choice, in the power of my own free will.

BAM! There it was. Control. *Well, this is happening,* I thought. There is no running from Holy Spirit when He starts to put the smack down on control versus free will.

In my free will, I was still choosing to control the narrative, in the form of holding onto this hand and the ability to choose when it would get played, when I would get pay-back, and against whom.

Now, in my free will, He was asking me to choose to *surrender control* back to Him and throw more chips on the table, by trusting Him with what had become so precious to me: the winning. In order to gain greater freedom in the future, I needed to now learn to surrender, to be grateful and humble—to submit, to trust. This was a major redefinition of how I understood what it meant to "hold the winning hand."

He knew me better than I knew myself. He was asking me to give Him back the hands of time and of timing that He gave me when He created the foundations of the earth, the sun and the moon. Because, when you really think about it, control is an illusion and is the opposite of free will.

This step wasn't very easy for me, because everything already seemed so out-of-control at that point in my life. My trust in my life situations was so deeply broken. So, to surrender the one thing I felt I *could* control took a lot of trust.

On the bright side though, He also showed me He would hold the winning hand close to *His* heart and that His heart was uncompromising in love for me. By holding it in His heart, this caused my heart to turn away from the poker table towards Him. I saw how it was His grace that had given me this hand to hold onto. He knew what was coming and what I would need to get me through it. I also needed to trust Him now that He was asking for it back because He knew what was coming still and I didn't. The control that I thought I needed to get me to this place would only hurt me more than surrendering would.

I think the greatest lesson I learned through this experience is to trust that I don't always know everything, even when I think I do. I need to always allow room for the Holy Spirit to lead, guide and direct—even when it seems the opposite is occurring. To me, this is what His sovereignty is: He knows what, when, where, how and why. I can always trust His sovereignty over my own ability to control the outcome. This was my major redefining revelation. And all this came through journaling my holy imagination, asking questions, and allowing Holy Spirit to adjust my thinking.

My need for control is what brought me to the place where all those chips were being thrown down. I had believed the lies of the enemy and they had taken hold—including the lie that I needed to be in control.

I had taken the winning hand God had given me and turned it into something that made me feel that I was still able to control my life when everything felt out of control. But *His sovereignty* was the trump card I would catch "in the river" that would truly give me the winning hand.

the WINNING HAND

Remember This Principle When....

- You find yourself daydreaming and you don't know if there is a deeper meaning.

- You find yourself full of emotions and need to get them out.

- You are learning to listen to your spirit.

- You have a dream or vision that you want to go back to later.

CHAPTER 10

CREATING
a bubble

Journal excerpt: It's 4 a.m. and tears are flowing. My heart is swelling up, then spilling out my eyes. Joy, gratitude, love, pain and fear all mix together, like a carbonated can being shaken together and then opened. It's messy—yet not totally unexpected, at the same time.

It's in these moments I remember that I am loved right where I am. These are the moments when the tension of "who I'm not at this moment" meets "who I am becoming" through my experiences. It's that place where I am challenged, through the tension and the shaking, to grow and change. It's a choice between having the grace to grow, expand and mature, or to remain at my current capacity.

I have never been more grateful than I am in these moments of the woman I have become. Of the strength I know that, without a doubt, I have obtained through the battles I have faced.

Yet my heart and soul can sometimes still scream, *When is it my turn to be weak? When is it my turn to have someone fight for me? When will I have a moment to be safe enough to take off my armor and set it aside for a minute? When can I have a second to take down my guard and receive the comfort I long for? Can't anyone see the dings in my armor that threaten to leave me with a gaping hole?*

The self-pity, the anger, the "what about me" scream from a place where it seems no one hears. It screams that there is a person with a heart, love, and pain under all this armor.

The voice on the outside says, "I got this—I can do this a little longer." But the voice on the inside is saying, *I need reprieve—I need to hit the pause button and regroup. Can't you just give me one second?* And yet, I keep going. I keep picking up that sword and going forward without reprieve. *Why?*

How do I stop and take off the armor, when I still have a desire in my heart for more?

My head is swirling, my heart is achy, and my spirit—my guiding light, my core being—well, I don't even hear it anymore.

I need time. Time to adjust, time to grieve what was, time to tend to the dents in the armor I've taken on in such a short time. Time to listen to my spirit and be renewed and refreshed. I really need time to rest and connect, spirit-to-Spirit.

But when? I keep telling myself, *One more day, maybe Monday night? Maybe Tuesday? Oh wait, I can't then, I have something that day.* And next thing I know, a week has passed. The pile gets higher and the dings keep coming. Red warning flags start popping up everywhere.

The real red flag warning is telling me, "Stop and re-evaluate what you are doing."

Jesus was so self-aware, yet also aware of the needs of the people. In one instance, He left the crowd and all the people and went away to have time to regroup, to rest his body, soul and spirit. But that didn't mean He was weak, incapable, or unable to sustain. He just had healthy boundaries for Himself and others. He flowed with the Spirit and didn't give into religious ways with others or Himself. Caring for others *and* self-care were both equally worthy of His time and attention.

Harmony is so very important to my well-being. Allowing each note of my experience to be heard and to work together—body, soul, heart and spirit. When one note takes over the rhythm of life's heartbeat, life can lose the beauty of the song. When that happens, it takes time and intentionality to correct it, before the off-beats start to sound right again. Otherwise, the symphony of sound will be lost in the chaos, and the steady tick-tock of the metronome changes to something that no longer flows or sounds right.

So here I sit—my heart spilling out of my eyes in the quiet of the 4 a.m. stillness—recognizing that the beat is off, that my reflection is starting to become unrecognizable, and that it's time for self-care.

No one else can take off my armor, no one else can mend the dents, no one else can give me strength and the rest I need but me—and it's a choice. I can keep fighting and keep going, waiting for rescue. However, whoever comes to rescue me will become my Savior—and I already have one of those living inside me. It's time to go meet with Him in my "bubble."

***

When I went through a recovery program from drug and alcohol abuse, I had some pretty disturbing memories come up, as I've mentioned earlier. It was also during this time that I was told I had PTSD. It became hard for me to sort through what was real and what wasn't. Life felt like a roller coaster. People I knew would go to put their arm around me and I would flinch and cower in a knee-jerk reaction.

As memories continued to surface, the emotions began to make connections. Things I thought and believed felt like ingredients, all mixed together and put in a pressure cooker, ready to explode. I could be downright irrational and overreact to the littlest things. Sleep was elusive, which just added fuel to the already unstable atmosphere I found myself in.

That's when I learned that I could create a "safe space" in my thinking and go there anytime I wanted. The bubble is also another example of when I use holy imagination. But this "bubble" principle has become such a profound experience for me that it's become its own tool that I use regularly.

I am a very visual person, so back then I would picture a place that made me feel safe that was also empty: no people, nothing to cause fear, no excess noise. Anything I didn't want there didn't make the cut and wasn't allowed to come in this space. I could add to or take away anything I wanted to, at any time. It was my safe place—or, as I later termed it, my "bubble."

My "bubble" was a garden, pulled from my mind and connected to Psalm 23. It had a bench by a brook that created a quiet, constant, soothing sound for me. Generally, it was always sunny, yet cool there. At times, a fog of protection, like a thick blanket, would roll in. There have been times when it was sunset, times when it was sunrise. I could hear the occasional sound from a wild animal, but it was always peaceful. Its peace was the most important part for me.

Over time, my bubble has changed and expanded. It has now become almost a way of life where peace rules, love is abundant, and patience is just a breath away. If you haven't guessed it yet, my bubble is also my "abiding place." It is where my soul and spirit go to commune with God, heal, and be free. It's the very heart of who I am as a person. It was the trauma and the turmoil that *wasn't* me. They were a side effect of what had been done to me.

You want to know the best part about my bubble? I can always be in vacation mode, no matter where I am. That's my fav!

I pull from memories of moments on vacations where I have been able to just sit back and breathe it all in. Moments like when I was on a cruise, sitting on a chair outside, the sun had just set and there, in the openness of the Atlantic Ocean, the stars began to shine. I felt like I was in a dome, totally protected by beauty. That has become my staple atmosphere in my bubble: "vacay mode." I bring vacation mode *with* me, instead of needing to go somewhere to have to find it.

You want to know the other best part of it? **I can be there, no matter what is happening around me**. If I'm at home, cooking for my kid, and he is telling me I am the "worst Mom ever!"— dude, I'm cool because I am on vacation, so I have joy. If I fear finances might run out before the month does—awesome, I am at rest. If anxiousness pops up, or people are starting up drama around me—sweet, I have my bubble. If I get scared, lonely, or tired? My bubble has rest, love, and acceptance, and I am always allowed to abide there.

When I chat with Holy Spirit in my bubble, it can become an adventure, where He will take my hand and ask my permission to take me on a journey. He is ever the gentleman in respecting my free will. (I have said "no," to Him, but it never ends well. The "no" eventually dies and a "yes" is resurrected in its place, as Holy Spirit is patient to wait on me.)

I'll be honest, I didn't really think my bubble was a big deal. I am only writing about it because someone I love and trust said, "You should write about your bubble." So here I am, being a good friend, and you can all thank her if this is, like, your favorite thing *ever*.

As my bubble has become a more solid, tangible presence of peace, freedom, and self-love—as well as a place of healing, wholeness and truth—it has expanded. Have you ever just hung out with someone who brought you peace or motivated you? Someone who set your mind at ease? That same solid, tangible presence comes from this practice.

It's a Choice

Now here is the tricky part. It's a choice, and I'm always going to remind you of that. As my friend (who is always drilling this into my head the way I am drilling it into yours now) says, we have the freedom of choice. None of this really happens like a "poof!" magical moment. This is part of the journey of life. I had to *choose* to create this space. I had to choose to spend time there, I had to choose to build in it and to stay in it—to grow, add to and take away from it. Abiding is always there when I want it, yet it is also always a choice.

I would love to tell you that I live there all the time—but I don't. Recently, I was walking through some situations and wondering why things were getting to me in a way they hadn't in a while. I was feeling jaded and cynical, which really isn't like me anymore. Then I realized I hadn't been intentionally spending time in my bubble. It was time to upgrade and fortify it again. I had to spend time taking a look at what had seduced me away from it. (Time to see if my side of the street is clean. Again.)

Building a bubble doesn't mean you ignore negative emotions or reality, and opt for fantasy instead. It is not the absence of negative emotions. It means there is a safe space to process and work through negative emotions.

I can be at peace while I'm working through anger. I can have love when I feel rejection. I can be at peace even when there is drama happening around me. It definitely makes life easier when I actually remember to live from this place and not always feel like I am trying to "get there."

So, to learn to build a bubble, we can choose to pull from experiences with people, places, things, moments, and memories, bringing them into our current selves at any time. We can rest in that until the bubble becomes more tangible.

I find the best time to do this is before bed, when all is quiet except my mind. I find it's best to practice in these quiet spaces, without interruption, until it gets established. Then I can take it for a test drive in normal, every-day life. You can even set an alarm on your phone for certain times a day—whenever is convenient for you—that says "Bubble."

Funny thing is, when you start doing this, you will start to see and hear the word "bubble" everywhere. I can't explain why this happens—it just seems to happen to people. A friend of mine texted me a picture while she was at the park, because there were a bunch of kids there with bubble guns. She said, "When I forget, there are reminders everywhere." I love when people text me these things to help remind me, too.

When I first started practicing this, I didn't have "good" memories. I didn't have much to hold onto. I had my spirit and I had a healthy imagination that wasn't fantasy, so that's where I started. The garden that I imagined from Psalms 23 was my starting spot.

It took me a year or more before my bubble became truly real, as I added real-life moments of beauty to it. As I began to be grateful and appreciate things more, this added to it also. I have even created real-life moments to help the process, like the cruise ship after sunset. I will also take the time to go walk the beach by myself and enjoy a quiet sunset, and purposefully stop and draw from it. I will even take a picture, so that I can easily go back and scroll through my phone when I need to, in order to remember the moment.

Some nights I have shut off my phone, popped on headphones, sat outside and created a beautiful bubble moment. Taking a bath or even a long, hot shower on purpose, cleaning myself off of the weariness or turmoil of the day, also help me to get into "bubble mode." Sometimes, taking the time to find what you appreciate or are thankful for helps in accessing and creating a bubble. Start from a positive place. Building your bubble becomes a journey worth taking.

Another of my favorite parts about my bubble world? It's mine. It's my space, my heart, my joys, my version of what beauty is. I can also take off my armor in my bubble. There isn't any battle when you're abiding, only rest and peace. I don't have to fight, there is no war here. I carry rejuvenation with me in my bubble everywhere I go. And like I always say, if I don't remember to go there initially, I always end up there eventually.

I have a plaque on my wall that says: "I will create beautiful things and this will be my life." I think it's working.

CREATING *a bubble*

Remember This Principle When....

- You find yourself constantly battling negativity in or around you.

- You need peace and joy.

- You are dealing with flashbacks, panic, and/or anxiety.

- You are struggling to find peace in your current situation.

CHAPTER 11

removing the LANDING PAD

It is a "bubble" day for me, as I'm sitting on my hammock, doing some deep processing as I work out a question. I feel overwhelmed and frustrated at the tension I'm carrying from several challenges I'm facing all at once. In addition, I have heard some teaching that isn't sitting quite right, so I'm stirred up.

I suddenly hear the sound of a helicopter in my safe, "bubble" space. It is flying in circles, causing quite the disturbance: wind blowing, leaves flying everywhere. I ask Holy Spirit what is going on. He says the helicopter is looking for a landing pad. I don't like the sound of that. I don't want this noisy thing in my garden. *What landing pad? I don't have a landing pad here—this is a garden!* I thought.

This opens up a conversation I am not prepared for. I recognize all these disturbances vying for my attention. The lack of ease over the teaching, the friction and frustration I am feeling, are like a helicopter of turmoil entering my peace and my sense of joy and love. One that is trying to land and take up space in *my* garden.

"How do I get rid of the landing pad so that the helicopter will have no place to land?" I ask Holy Spirit. I want it to have to go land somewhere else, or run out of fuel. Holy Spirit and I walk over to the landing pad—the one that I didn't even know was there. There are people surrounding it, holding jackhammers, already tearing into it and breaking it apart. I see another crew pulverizing those pieces into dust.

"How and when did these people get here?" I ask. Holy Spirit proceeds to introduce me. "This is Peace. He has been here working at this for a while," He says. "This is Joy. You forgot about him for a while, but he never forgot about you. And this is Laughter, also known as Light-Hearted." He goes down the line and introduces me to all the attributes I have worked to become.

So here is peace, joy, beauty, appreciation, love, acceptance, grace and so much more, all chipping away at the landing pad of noise and confusion, anger and self-loathing that were causing me so much trouble.

"Well, why was the helicopter here then?" I ask.

Holy Spirit took me to the second crew, who were pulverizing the concrete to dust. As the helicopter would fly in a circle around the garden, the dust would fly everywhere and disappear.

"Sometimes, there's a purpose in it," Holy Spirit replies. "That helicopter is a disruption to you now, but before, you didn't even recognize its presence. You didn't notice what it was carrying with it. In fact," Holy Spirit continued, "You even looked forward to its arrival, because it had become your normal. There was a false sense of safety attached to its familiar annoyance.

"Now, not only are you able to recognize the helicopter's presence, but its presence also blows the dust of the landing pad away. You are no longer familiar with it and have even forgotten that the landing pad was here. The helicopter keeps coming to look for a place to land, yet it doesn't realize that every time it shows up, it's blowing away pieces of the very thing it needs to land. The noise and confusion it is trying to bring become a reminder of how much you have grown and healed. Because you recognize that, you also remember you don't want that kind of distraction to be able to land in your life again. So it actually is blowing away the possibility of it ever being able to take root again."

***

My sense of peace increased that day. I understood that I didn't need to fear, because the helicopter that was trying to bring all that trauma back actually had no place to land. It might go away to gas up and come back, looking again for a place to land, but eventually, it would stop. The helicopter might pass over on its way to somewhere else, yet I was free from it finding a place to land with me.

I learned I had a little more forgiveness to work on, as the helicopter's presence did get me stirred up, pulling me away from peace. But now I at least had the correct thinking to process its presence. Every time the helicopter makes a racket, I can be thankful, grateful and blessed at the reminder of how far I have come.

The awareness of the turmoil and noise—or even drama—is as much a part of growth as it being gone is. We can't heal from something that isn't revealed. My hope is that you begin to recognize when that noisy helicopter is there, not in order to give it a place to land, but to be grateful that you *have* recognized it. Now that you recognize it, you also can begin the journey of removing the landing pad.

I also hope that you find within these chapters ways to help demolish the landing place it is looking for—whatever that is for you. I hope that you realize one day (maybe even today) that there is more peace present, more joy, and more of my favorite, light-heartedness. My hope is that, as you grow your bubble and become more of who you were created to be, you will pass that freedom along to the next person.

removing the LANDING PAD

Remember This Principle When….

- You feel annoyed by drama or trauma trying to invade your peace.

- You can't figure out why you're not at rest.

- You feel like turmoil and triggers keep happening.

- You feel like you are going backwards and not moving forwards.

CHAPTER 12

red BALLOON

One day, not long before my son was born, I was sitting in my back yard just minding my own business when, in my imagination, I began to see a forest of trees with red balloons tied onto all the branches. As I'm looking into the picture, there are hundreds of red balloons on the trees, if not thousands. I instantly think of a counseling exercise I used to use.

I would have the client write on a helium balloon whatever weight they were carrying. Then they would hold onto a heavy brick with one hand, while holding the helium balloon in the other, which would be dancing around wanting to be free. Once the weight of the brick got to be too much, the counselee would let go of the brick and the balloon at the same time. The heavy brick would hit the ground, giving freedom to whatever had been weighing them down as it symbolically floated away with the balloon.

However, in the image I was now seeing, these red balloons were tied to trees. The first question that came to my mind was "How do you let go of a tree?"

I mean, wouldn't that be *your* first thought?

So, off I go with all my questions for Holy Spirit, because, you know, that's just weird! Why are the balloons tied to trees? Why are there so many red balloons? What's written on them? Why trees? Does this have anything to do with letting go? That's *a lot* of letting go!

Being who I am, this sets me off onto a path of deep and wide processing. Trees have roots, and the trees I saw were huge, like gigantic oak trees. They had lots of limbs, so there were lots of balloons on each tree. Like a lifetime of balloons. I hold onto this image and ponder on it. I look at it from different angles, asking questions that I try to answer.

(Yes, I talk to myself and yes, I answer myself as well. My ability to self-talk is amazing! My ability to self-answer has been an interesting journey. But I digress.)

Anyway, a few days go by and I wake up feeling a huge shift in my atmosphere, as if all of a sudden, the season had gone from a hot, heavy, humid Florida summer to a northern springtime. I feel light, free and clean—and yet now totally confused.

I don't mean to say the weather actually changed. I'm saying my own internal or spiritual atmosphere changed—just like that. The image I had then shifted as well, with those red balloons now floating away in the wind, set free from the limbs onto which they had been tied.

Then I hear this rising up in my spirit: "The Spirit is like the wind, you can't see it, but you can tell where it's going and what it's doing." This is from a verse in the Bible found in John 3:8. *The Passion Translation* of this verse puts it this way: "For the Spirit-Wind blows as it chooses. You can hear its sound, but you don't know where it came from or where it's going. So it is the same with those who are Spirit-born!" I like this version because it's closer to the way I heard this verse that day.

Suddenly, I could tell what the Spirit was wanting to do, because the balloons had been released and I could see where the Spirit-wind was taking them. I began to understand a little about why I suddenly felt light, clean, free—and yet confused.

Being me, I start offloading a ton of questions.

Filters

Instead of delving deep into a 2,000-page novel about how I came to understand this more, I'll just have some kindness here and take you to some of the revelation that came from it. (This is going to be fun, because I bet you'll start to see red balloons everywhere after this.)

The specific thing that Holy Spirit was highlighting to me had to do with how I had all these filters that were interfering with the destiny and direction of my life.

For example, I had encouraging words that people had shared with me about what they perceived God was doing in my life. I had similar words about what I thought God was doing. I also had all these teachings and various books with their authors' ideas. These all had become the "red balloons" with words written on them, but they were feeling like weights to me. I was tying these balloons to things in my life in the natural, based on what I thought they meant.

What is important to understand in this vision is that these words—which were actually meant to be helpful—had instead become weights. They went through my filters of what I thought was possible or what I thought I was qualified for. Sometimes, these were filtered through the negative words either spoken to me or that I believed about myself.

For instance, I once had someone tell me they saw me as the next Beth Moore or Joyce Meyer, which may have sounded encouraging to them. Well, I didn't want to be the next Beth or Joyce, no offense to them, of course. I am sure they are great people, but I had no desire to be like them. I thought (and here is the filter) that meant I would be standing in front of a bunch of people, all eyes on me, being scrutinized by the public, with people judging my walk with God. So, in essence, I had tied that "red balloon" to a tree in order to not let that happen. Instead of letting the filter go, I let it grow roots. Then I set out to become the opposite of that.

So, I stopped sharing a lot of the stuff I wrote. I also got upset when I was asked to speak and would attempt to sabotage myself. I didn't think I could be who they thought I could be.

It never occurred to me, back then, that maybe the person who told me about being the next Joyce Meyer or Beth Moore actually just meant that I would have a relationship with God that would help others to also have a relationship with Him. Like those two women do.

Here's another example of a red balloon, tied to the same tree. Throughout my life, I had people tell me over and over that they couldn't understand things I was saying or that I wrote. This was very contradictory to that other word about being like those two writers who were also speakers! So being misunderstood became another red balloon attached to a tree that had taken root. I always felt misunderstood and stupid.

So, all these red balloons in that picture stood for the weights I carried around with me. Present words, past words, present teachings, past teachings, books, songs—all of it, even scriptures, that I had tied all these meanings to, based on my filters of what I thought they meant.

Now there was a flip side to this. (Stay with me, I'm going somewhere.)

If I am tying all these red balloons to trees, then they are essentially weighed down, stuck and they don't have the opportunity to go where they are meant to—up, away and wherever the Spirit-wind wanted to take them. So, my meaning and definition of them had no freedom to move, to change, or to go anywhere. Therefore, this kept *me* from moving, changing and having freedom.

Also, everything I heard and experienced would be filtered through whatever I had that red balloon tied to. For example, if someone told me I was a good writer or teacher, I would think, "No, that's not possible. I'm misunderstood, stupid and I don't want to be like Joyce Meyer or Beth Moore."

Therefore, I was limiting the move of Spirit-wind in my own life. Because, as I've mentioned, since we have free will and the power of choice, the Spirit-wind couldn't move the balloons that I had tied down to the trees.

Another word for this, in a nutshell, is "misinterpretation." I had misinterpreted things that I had heard and read, and those misinterpretations led to me misunderstanding who I really was. Here we go on another redefining moment! I needed to redefine what it meant for me to be a good writer or teacher. It didn't have to look like anyone else. It could look like me.

Words are powerful, in the same way that a lack of words is also powerful.

So, do I always remember now to let the red balloons fly freely away? *Pppfffttt*, no. Do I always recognize what filters I still have? Nope! I do, however, hear the Holy Spirit a little quicker when He tells me to look for a "red balloon."

Just like the brick being dropped and the helium lifting that balloon away, when I do recognize it, I can feel that same "season-change" freedom, and I no longer have the weight of that filter limiting me. I recognize it for what it is and let it go.

So, here I am, decades later, writing a book, not letting filters get in the way of my destiny and dreams for my life. And here you are reading because, I believe, you want the same thing. You have hopes, desires, and dreams and it's time to set them free.

red BALLOON

Remember This Principle When….

- You begin to wonder if you're limiting yourself.

- You feel an inexplicable weight.

- You don't feel free to be your full self.

- You feel unqualified.

CHAPTER 13

LOVED *healing* WHOLE

Say this with me:
I am loved.
I am healing.
I am whole.

Our journey together is coming to a close. This chapter won't be like the others. As you have seen, this book has introduced you to a little bit of my journey. Maybe you can relate, and hopefully you have heard a little of your own journey in mine. Maybe you heard the journey of a friend or loved one. Maybe it has ignited in you the desire for a new journey. Maybe this even gives you the hope to keep going, knowing that you are not alone.

Along my journey, one big stumbling block I have faced over and over is the idea that, "I am the only one." The only one who struggles. The only one who faces "demons" of negative self-talk and the fear of rejection. I feared that others would see me and how screwed-up I was and would run for the hills. *Because obviously, no one else could be as screwed up as me*, I thought.

I thought I was the only one like this, who just couldn't "get it." Why do I fall, get up, fall, and get up again? Why do I repeat this pattern?

Yes, I got off the street, but I ended up in a relationship of domestic violence. I got out of the domestic violence, but I was still doing drugs and drinking. I got off the drugs and alcohol, but I still struggled with PTSD. I was healing from PTSD, but I still struggled with religiosity and spirituality. I was learning to heal from religion, but still struggled with rejection. I thought I was alone in feeling like I was always climbing out of some hole, seeking to be whole.

You are not alone. You are loved right where you are.

Love isn't always a feeling, sometimes it's a choice. Ultimately, Love, for me, is a person in the form of Jesus. Because of His love, I choose to love everyone who reads this book the best that I can. So, you are loved by me.

Why? How? Because it's my love that wrote these words. My love for those who need help, just like I did, and still do. My love for those who helped me to get to where I am today. I wouldn't be here without their love. I want to love in the same way that I have been loved. My love for myself and the journey that got me here gives me the love I have for others on their journey.

Writing this book has been the best way I could find to express this love to you and let you know that you are not alone and you are loved.

Which Came First?

Say this with me again: "I am loved. I am healing. I am whole."

That last one is hard, isn't it?

I am whole.

"How can I be healing and also already be whole?" you may be asking.

The simple answer? Because you are loved right where you are.

Which came first, being loved, healing or being whole? What if you are whole already and that is how you receive being loved right where you are? What if you are whole and that wholeness is what is causing the healing?

What if being loved, and being whole could be like the bread that holds the sandwich meat of healing in place? I don't know the answer to these questions, but it's these questions that led me to realizing I am loved, healing, and I am already whole, and on a journey to realizing what it means to be whole.

I have learned that nothing I have done or that's been done to me ever prevented me from being whole. It just prevented me from *seeing* that I was whole. That's where the healing comes in.

Writing this has been just as much a journey of healing for me as I hope reading it has been for you.

We all need people and tools to help us. My hope is that you take these tools and learn to apply them to your own life, your own relationships, and your own areas of struggle. Make them yours. Then you share them with others, in your own way.

We all have a voice. My hope is that this book is enough of a spark to ignite you to be the spark that ignites others.

I am loved, healing, and whole, helping others to be loved, healing, and whole. Just like you are loved, healing, and whole, helping others be loved, healing and whole. It's reciprocal. So, which came first, the chicken or the egg? Does it matter, when we have both a chicken and an egg?

LOVED *healing* WHOLE

Remember This Principle When….

- You feel like giving up.

- You think healing seems never-ending.

- You feel like you are the only one struggling.

- You are isolating and feeling broken.

CHAPTER 14

WELCOME TO
your future

I wrote this whole book to say, "Welcome to your future."

Pffeewww! I didn't think I could hold that in for another second.

This is about *your* future now.

It's a hilarious story to me, the way this idea of "Welcome to your future" came to be.

I had a new friend I was hanging out with, during that sometimes awkward "getting to know you" curve. Sometimes my son would come with me to hang out with my new friend. My son, like all kids, would occasionally have a meltdown while we were out trying to enjoy our day. After my son and I had worked through it and were on the other side of the meltdown, I would look at my friend and say, "Welcome to your future." Or, when my son and I would get into some crazy shenanigans, I would say to my friend, "Welcome to your future."

I said this as a way of saying, "If we are going to continue to be friends, this is what you are getting yourself into."

Well, one day as I was tending to my kid and feeling overwhelmed, I was carrying a bunch of bags while also helping my son carry all his stuff. My friend grabbed all of that stuff out of my hands, looked at me and said, "Welcome to your future."

I almost started crying. I felt those words in my spirit and in my heart, my core being.

Here I was offering my friend what I considered to be my very hectic life, and my friend just said back to me, "Here I am, offering you help with your very hectic life."

Of course, Holy Spirit has had just the best time with this. So, I am going to pose it to you like this, and see if together, we can welcome you to your future.

Welcome to your future, where you are loved right where you are.

Welcome to your future that stays on the side of truth, with no more lies.

Welcome to your future, where your side of the street is clean and fresh.

Welcome to your future, where you are looking out the windshield.

Welcome to your future, with wayfinding signs to help you navigate.

Welcome to your future, where you have on your oxygen mask.

Welcome to your future, where you have a lower your pain tolerance, so there is less pain to tolerate.

Welcome to your future, redefined. (Whoa! That one even hits me right in the heart.)

Welcome to your future, where you can journal and explore your holy imagination and all the insights it holds.

Welcome to your future, where you have a bubble to abide in.

Welcome to your future, where you no longer have a landing pad for turmoil.

Welcome to your future, where you can release your red balloons and be free.

Welcome to your future, where you are loved, healing, and whole.

Welcome to your future, where you can welcome your future, and it is no longer a repeat of your past.

Just like my friend came to help me with my baggage, you have these tools from a friend to help you with your baggage. Your future has help.

There was a time in my life that my future wasn't very bright. I didn't even think my future would extend beyond my teen years. I never celebrated my birthday because I didn't see the point. Why celebrate my birth? There was a huge chasm between the life I had always known and what I thought life was supposed to be: full of love, hope, beauty and intimacy. I had lost faith in what I couldn't see: Love. But Love picked me up, over and over and over. That's what love does. It never fails. It never gives up. You may not *feel love,* but that doesn't mean you aren't loved.

So, welcome to your future. Welcome to the journey into your future.

Your future. Not your past—that is just a rearview image. Welcome to your future where, if you are carrying your past, you can stop at a rest area. Where you can fortify your bubble, and have peace within you.

Welcome to **your** future.

WELCOME TO *your future*

Remember This Principle When….

- You need a boost in confidence.

- You need some encouragement.

- You think you are losing faith.

- You fear the past repeating itself.

WHAT'S NEXT?

You may be wondering, "What's next? What do I do now that I have read all this?"

You can soak in it, read and reread. Answer some of the questions in each chapter. Learn to apply the truth of each chapter to your life. Take your time and don't rush. Pick two or three chapters that resonated with you the most and just start there.

A friend read this and gave me feedback. He said "If someone could get just one or two of these principles and really apply it, that would cause transformation." I think he is right.

This book was meant to be a stand-alone resource.

However, if you want more, I will be offering *Digging Deeper* sessions online where people can come together and we can dig into each chapter a little more, like a book club. You can just join the sessions you want as they are available. Then if you still want more, I will also offer one-on-one *Deeper Still* sessions for those who want a one-on-one focused look at a chapter.

All of this and more can be found on the website:

www.lovedhealingwhole.com.

INFLUENCES AND RESOURCES

Influences

These are some things that worked for me and things I "tried on" on my journey that may fit you or they may not, and that's ok. Find what fits you.

I will start with Graces Spaces and Allison Bown. Allison has written several wonderful books and has an online community that you will read more about below. One thing I learned from her, both personally and from her book *Joyful Intentionality* is that we each have a unique identity, so not everything should be a "one-size-fits-all" approach. That's why I offer the following as "influences," rather than pointing you to specific programs.

Recovery: I went to a recovery program for 10 months that included both Alcoholics Anonymous and Narcotics Anonymous. During this program, we often gave our testimony within varied groups of people and worked through a lot of inner healing. The one I attended had a residential work program as well. All of these things were wonderful influences for me. Some were just for a season, and some are with me for the long-term.

Healing Prayer: I was part of healing prayer ministry as a prayer minister. This both brought me healing and also helped me to hone hearing my spirit and Holy Spirit. The training alone was an invaluable experience for me.

Coaching: I was also part of an online community with teaching, coaching and training. Again, this was an invaluable season in my life where I gained a stronger voice and got more used to building community online, something new to this dinosaur.

I have also been to Al-Anon, therapy, counselors, mental health counselors and more. There are not many avenues I haven't utilized, actually. I can't say any specific one of them got me to where I am today, or that there is any one of them that I wish I hadn't done, because they were all steps on my journey.

Resources

Grace Spaces is a Christian coaching and training community founded by Allison Bown, CPLC. Grace Spaces honors that each of us processes and expresses life as a New Creation in Christ in many different and wonderful ways, and helps you to discover yours. That's why a one-size-fits-all process towards maturity rarely works.

Grace Spaces group coaching teams are 12 women or less, so that you practice with teammates who become friends. Together, you'll discover how God created you uniquely to experience life in Jesus, the strengths He's given you and His perspective for your vulnerabilities. Personal Coaching also available.

http://www.gracespaces.org/

Graham Cooke is a wonderful resource also. He has written a number of books and has many teaching series that have been pivotal in changing my mindsets and overcoming negativity. His work is also where I first met Allison Bown, and for that I will forever be grateful.

James Wilder is another amazing author whose books have had a profound impact one me and they are small and easy to read, and I'm grateful for that. He co-authored *Living From The Heart Jesus Gave You.*

Three more authors I will recommend actually write fiction. While I know that may seem odd, I am all about using the Holy Imagination, and these three have it in spades.

Charles Martin wrote *When Crickets Cry, The Dead Don't Dance,* and *The Water Keeper.* Just to make sure you have the correct author. I have read every book of his, and they're all amazing.

Ted Dekker wrote *The 49th Mystic,* and *Rise of the Mystics,* and the accompanying study books, which are amazing.

Francine Rivers is author of the *Mark of the Lion* series and *Redeeming Love,* which were life-changing novels for me.

A note for writers:

My editor and book coach, **Meg Mittelstedt**, is priceless. Her wisdom, patience, encouragement and teaching skills shaped and formed my voice in a very short time. I discovered that for me, writing and being an author are two very different things. Meg carried me from one to the other with absolute grace. Whether you are a writer or an already-established author, she is an amazing resource.

Meg's book coaching business is **Inkforge Book Coaching**, at inkforge.ca. She helps writers to understand and navigate the process of creating a publishable manuscript, including assessing chapter topics, creating writing prompts, the writing process, outlining, book structure, manuscript flow, storytelling, showing versus telling, and much, much more.

NOTION Design Group, including Kailey Kisabeth and Ryan Parker, took what was in my heart and handed it back to me in the form of graphics. I literally cried the first time they showed me their ideas. They are attentive and the framework they use to build logos, websites and other resources is incomparable to anything else on offer out there for businesses.

As a newbie in both of these areas, I was grateful to have had both of these small businesses by my side to help me walk out my dreams and make them a reality.